STEP-BY-STEP

CHICKEN

COOKBOOK

EDITED BY SUSAN TOMNAY

CRESCENT BOOKS
NEW YORK

CONTE

Almond Chicken with Brandy Sauce, page 72

Crispy Tomato and Onion Chicken, page 30

Roast Chicken with Bacon and Sage Stuffing, page 31

Garlic Chicken Kebabs with Tomato and Mushroom Salad, page 40.

Chicken Burgers with Brown Mustard Cream, page 35

Camembert Chicken with Cranberry Sauce, page 66

The Publisher thanks the following for their assistance in the photography for this book: Barbara's Storehouse; Corso de' Fiori; Country Floors; Home and Garden on the Mall; Inmaterial; I. Redelman & Son; IVV; Krosno; Made on Earth; Mikasa Tableware; Noritake; Pacific East India Company Paraphenalia; Royal Doulton; Villeroy & Boch.

Baked Chicken Rolls, page 89

Chicken and Pepperoni Pasta, page 108

Step-by-Step

When we test our recipes we rate them for ease of preparation.

A single symbol indicates a recipe that is simple and generally quick to make—perfect for beginners.

Two symbols indicate the need for just a little more care and a little more time.

Three symbols indicate special dishes that need more investment in time, care and patience—but the results are worth it.

Front cover: Lemon and Rosemary Chicken, page 68.
Inside front cover: Tandoori Chicken Skewers and Chili Chicken with Salsa, page 38.
Inside back cover: Chicken Burgers with Brown Mustard Cream, page 35.

Chicken Basics

Chicken is a versatile food—it lends itself to many different recipes
and styles of cuisine. This guide to purchasing, storing, cooking and presentation
will help you prepare successful and delicious chicken dishes.

Let's talk about how to get the best out of chicken: what you should look for when buying chicken and how to store and prepare your chicken before cooking. We will also tell you how to make chicken broth, the art of carving, and wines to accompany your meal.

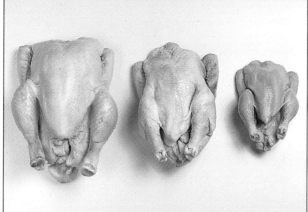

The three basic chicken sizes: (from left to right) large boiling fowl; roasting chicken; baby (squab) chicken or poussin.

The young roaster is 6–8 lb and the capon is 8–10 lb.

Whole chickens are sold cleaned, with innards removed. The chicken's neck is usually tucked inside. Sometimes the giblets are in the cavity, in a bag, so be sure to remove them before cooking or freezing. Giblets weigh between 1/4–1/2 lb. Be sure to consider this when determining the weight of the chicken and the number of portions you will get after cooking. Look for skin that is light pink and moist, unbroken and free from blemishes or bruises. The breast should be plump and well-rounded; on a young bird the point of the breastbone will be flexible. At specialty poultry shops you can buy free-range, grain-fed, and corn-fed chickens, which have yellow skin and flesh. Chicken can also be purchased cooked. Hot take-out barbecue, roast or char-grilled chicken has become a timesaver for many

PURCHASING

There is a wide variety of chickens and chicken cuts available in today's market. Young tender chickens, 2½–3½ lb, are good for grilling, frying, stir-frying, and roasting. Chickens over 3½ lb are suitable for braising or stewing because of their less-tender flesh, although they have excellent flavor. Unless you specifically want a very large or a very small bird, the 2½–3½ lb chicken is the most readily available in today's market, and can serve many purposes.

Whole baby chickens, or poussins, weigh about 1 lb or less and are generally considered to be one serving. A more common bird of this size is the Cornish Hen. Cornish hens are young hens with a direct blood-line to the British poultry breed Cornish. They weigh 1–1½ lb and are considered to be two servings.

Broiler-fryers are 2½–4 lb and come whole, cut up, or packaged by piece; sometimes boned and skinned. The stewing hen generally weights 4½–6 lb. It is best suited for roasting or stewing.

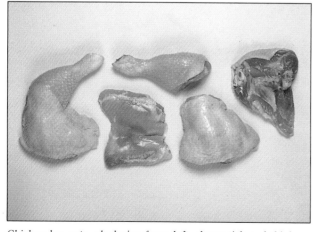

Chicken leg cuts, clockwise from left, drumstick-and-thigh, drumstick, thigh (underside view), thigh cutlet, thigh fillet.

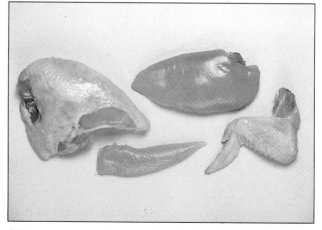

Chicken breast and wing cuts, clockwise from left, whole breast with bone, single breast fillet, wing, tenderloin.

busy people and a helpful start to family meals (see page 100). Cooked chicken is available, whole or cut into pieces, from most delicatessens and supermarkets.

Chicken cuts include: double or single breasts on the bone, with skin or without; boneless, skinned chicken breast halves; tenderloin (the small strip of tender meat just behind the breast); chicken leg (the whole thigh and leg); thigh, boneless thighs, wings and drumsticks (bottom part of the leg). A broiler-fryer, cut up, usually includes 10 pieces; 2 drumsticks, 2 thighs, 2 wings, 2 breast halves and 2 back pieces.

Chicken is versatile and it is not always necessary to buy the most expensive pieces to produce an excellent result. You can save considerably on the cost by doing some of the work yourself, for example, buying a whole chicken and cutting it up yourself or buying whole chicken breasts and then halving, boning and skinning the breasts yourself.

Cuts used in this book include:

For roasting - whole chickens, weighing around $2\frac{1}{2}$–$3\frac{1}{2}$ lb broiler-fryers, whole or half breasts, wings, legs, drumsticks and thighs.

For grilling - chicken halves and quarters, wings, whole breasts, half breasts, drumsticks, legs, thighs or tenderloin.

For pan or stir-frying - boneless breasts, boneless thighs or tenderloin.

For deep-frying - drumsticks, wings, thighs, chicken pieces.

For braising or poaching - chicken pieces, either boneless or bone-in pieces.

For stock - wings, backs, bones, necks, giblets, stewing hens.

Storing fresh chicken: Chicken should be returned to a refrigerator as quickly as possible after purchase. Do not allow to remain in a warm place such as in a hot car or truck. The longer food is kept at temperatures between 40°F and 130°F, the greater the chance of harmful bacteria that could result in food poisoning.

Careful handling and thorough cooking is essential for the healthy and safe preparation of all chicken. 97% of all foodborne illness outbreaks are due to improper food handling and preparation. Prevalent factors are inadequate cooking, improper holding temperature and contaminated preparation equipment.

Follow these recommendations and guidelines:

Keep chicken refrigerated or frozen until ready to cook. Thaw in refrigerator or microwave, not out on your kitchen counter.

Keep raw poultry separate from other foods. Wash working surfaces, cutting boards, utensils, and hands after touching raw poultry.

Cook chicken thoroughly. Bone-in pieces or whole chickens should reach an internal temperature of 180°F in a meaty part, not touching bone. Juices should run clear, not pink. Boneless pieces should be cooked to an internal temperature of 165°F with no pink remaining.

Hot foods should maintain a temperature of 140°F or above. Cold foods should maintain a temperature of 140°F or below.

Before storing uncooked

chicken, discard the tight plastic wrappings and pour off any juices. Remove neck and giblets from birds. Giblets should be cooked immediately or stored separately. Use the neck and giblets for stock; chop the liver to flavor a sauce, gravy or stuffing. Rinse chicken well; loosely wrap in plastic wrap or place in a plastic bag. Seal well and refrigerate. A fresh, cleaned and wrapped chicken can be stored in the refrigerator for up to two days.

Storing cooked chicken: chicken should stand no more than an hour at room temperature after cooking. If keeping longer than this, store loosely wrapped in the refrigerator and use within three days. If the chicken has a sauce or stuffing, it should be eaten within 24 hours. Stuffing and gravy should be stored separately.

FROZEN CHICKEN

Make sure that any frozen chicken you buy from the supermarket freezer section is solid and completely enclosed in its packaging. Uncooked, home-frozen chicken will keep up to 6 months if in good condition. Remove giblets before freezing as they will begin to deteriorate after 8 weeks. If a package has partly defrosted it must never be refrozen; defrost fully in the refrigerator and cook promptly.

Stuffed birds should not be frozen, as stuffing will not freeze quickly enough to prevent development of harmful bacteria. If stuffing is to be frozen, store in a separate container in the freezer.

To freeze uncooked chicken, wrap in heavy duty plastic bags.

To freeze cooked dishes, place into plastic or aluminum containers.

Trim any pockets of fat from the chicken cavity before cooking.

Freezing fresh chicken: Have freezer temperature at 0°F or lower. Use heavy gauge freezer bags and good quality freezer plastic wrap to package fresh chicken. Label each package with details of contents, the date it was packaged and the unfrozen weight, using a waterproof pen. It is important to expel as much air as possible from packaging; oxygen left behind will speed up the process of oxidization of any fat, resulting in an unpleasant taste. If you do a lot of freezing, it may be worthwhile investing in a vacuum freezer pump to efficiently expel air. Secure freezer bags by twisting the open end and closing with masking tape. Never re-freeze thawed, uncooked poultry. Whole birds can be prepared for stuffing or cooking before freezing.

Freezing cooked chickens: Cooked whole chicken or pieces can be frozen with or without bones, for up to 2 weeks. After this time it will tend to dry out.

Moist chicken dishes such as casseroles, stews, curries and soups are all suitable for freezing. Cool completely in refrigerator. Spoon into airtight freezer containers; seal, label and freeze. As a general rule, freeze cooked chicken for a maximum of two months.

Defrosting: Frozen chicken must be completely thawed in the refrigerator before cooking; allow 2–3 hours per lb. A frozen bird should be cooked within 12 hours of thawing. Do not thaw chicken at room temperature. Microwave defrosting is not recommended for

STUFFING AND TRUSSING

Make the stuffing according to the recipe. Spoon the stuffing mixture into the tail cavity, filling loosely to allow for expansion during cooking. Secure the skin across the cavity with a skewer, or truss the bird as described below. Stuffing can also be pushed under the skin of the breast and into the neck cavity.

Trussing, or securing a whole bird with string, keeps in the stuffing and holds the bird compactly, so that legs or wing tips do not overcook, and so that the cooked bird sits neatly for carving.

After stuffing, pull the skin down over the opening. Turn the bird onto its breast and tie a long length of string right around the wings, securing them neatly. Turn the bird over, taking the string over the legs and crossing it under the chicken. Tuck the tail into the cavity and tie the legs together. After the chicken has been cooked and left to rest for 10 minutes, remove the trussing, then carve.

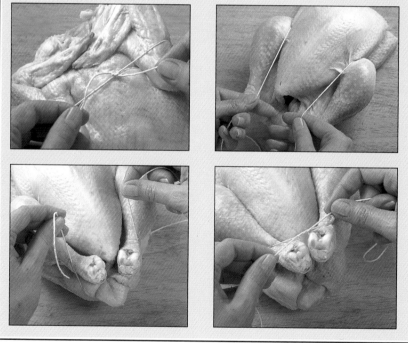

whole frozen chickens because of uneven thawing. However, smaller packages of chicken pieces or pre-cooked chicken can be successfully thawed in the microwave using the defrost setting. Always remove from wrapping before defrosting. Stir casseroles occasionally to

distribute heat evenly. Separate pieces as they thaw.

PREPARATION

Before cooking a whole chicken remove neck, giblets and pockets of fat from the cavity. Discard fat,

To remove skin from drumsticks, carefully loosen skin at the joint end.

Pull the skin back and away from the flesh of the drumstick.

a layer just underneath the skin. The skin can be removed before or after cooking. To remove skin from drumsticks, use a small sharp knife. Begin by carefully loosening skin from the flesh at the large joint end. Then pull down and away from the flesh. Poultry shears may prove helpful for skinning chicken also. Chicken breast halves and thighs are often available already skinned at stores.

use neck and giblets for broth. Remove excess fat from chicken pieces. Rinse poultry; pat dry with paper towels before cooking. Use a boning knife for cutting up whole uncooked chickens. Poultry shears are also helpful for dividing whole chickens into serving portions or halving Cornish hens.

Stuffing a whole chicken before roasting adds flavor and plumps up the bird. Do not stuff a bird more than two hours before cooking. If using warm stuffing, cook the bird immediately. Stuffed birds take a little longer to cook than unstuffed.

Some people prefer chicken without the skin. Removing the skin eliminates much of the fat from the chicken, as the fat lies in

Boning a chicken is a technique used for special-occasion dishes. With bones removed, chicken makes a meaty casing for a luxurious stuffing and the cooked bird is easy to carve or slice. Chicken presented in this way is often served cold. Chicken wings can also be boned and stuffed, making an easy-to-eat appetizer or finger food for parties.

JOINTING

Jointing a whole chicken is an easy process, once you know how. Large birds can be cut into 4, 6, 8 or 10 pieces. Use a sharp, heavy knife or poultry shears.

To cut a bird into 6 pieces, remove the leg by cutting around the end of the thigh joint. Twist the leg sharply outwards to break the thigh joint, and then cut through the joint. Turn the bird around and repeat on the other side. Remove wings by bending outwards and snipping

around the joint. Cut up one side of the body and open it out flat. Cut the body into 2 pieces. Cut down the center of the breast.

To make 8 portions, separate the thigh from the drumstick. To make 10 portions, cut the breast pieces in half. Always keep in mind that the dark meat of a chicken (legs and thighs) takes longer to cook than the white meat of a chicken (breasts).

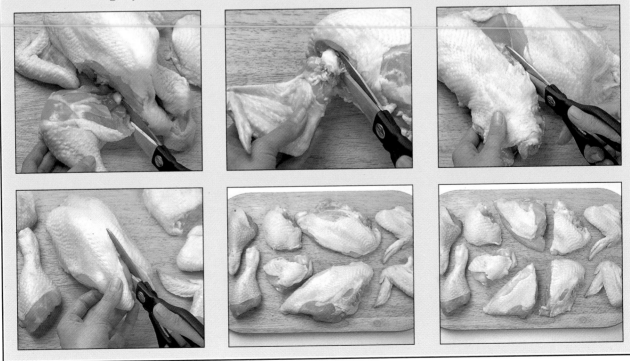

To marinate, pour liquid over the chicken in a non-metallic dish.

Marinating chicken gives it extra flavor and moisture. Marinades usually contain at least one acid ingredient such as wine, vinegar, lemon juice or yogurt, to tenderize, plus ingredients to flavor and color the chicken. Marinating is ideal to use in conjunction with quick-cooking methods. Frozen chicken should be thawed before marinating.

Place chicken in a shallow non-metal container and pour the marinade over. Turn chicken pieces to coat evenly. Cover with plastic wrap and refrigerate, usually for at least 2–8 hours, or overnight, turning occasionally. When ready to cook, drain the chicken and reserve or discard marinade, according to the particular recipe. The reserved marinade contains raw chicken juices and should not be used without cooking it. Brushing it on the chicken as the chicken cooks or boiling it in a sauce makes it safe to use. Honey or sugar should be used sparingly in marinades because sugary mixtures burn easily during cooking.

COOKING TECHNIQUE

Chicken must always be thoroughly cooked. To test when roasted or grilled poultry is cooked, insert a thermometer into the thickest part of the bird (the thigh). The internal temperature should reach 180°F and the juices run clear when the chicken is done. You can also test for doneness by twisting or jiggling the leg. If it moves easily in its socket, the chicken is cooked. Another test is to make a cut into the thickest

BONING WHOLE CHICKEN

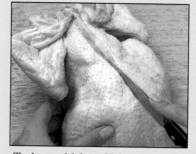 

To bone chicken: Using a small, sharp knife, cut through the skin on the center back. Separate the flesh from the bone down one side to the breast, being careful not to pierce skin. Follow along the bones closely with the

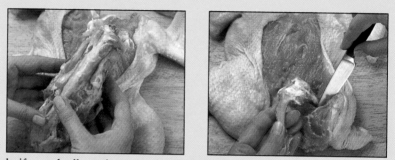

knife, gradually easing meat from thigh, drumstick and wing. Cut through thigh bone and cut off wing tip. Repeat on the other side, then lift the rib cage away, leaving the flesh in one piece. Scrape all the meat from the

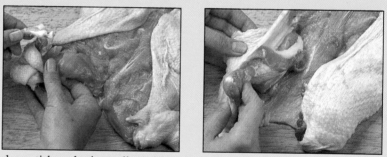

drumstick and wings; discard bones. Turn the wing and drumstick flesh inside the chicken and lay chicken out flat, skin-side down. The chicken is now ready to be stuffed and rolled according to the recipe.

part of the meat all the way to the bone. The meat is cooked when no pink remains near the bone and juices are clear, not pink.

There are two basic cooking methods—dry heat or moist heat. **Dry heat cookery** includes oven roasting, grilling, broiling, stir-frying and pan-frying. With these methods, juices are sealed in and the chicken is cooked quickly without the need for additional liquid during cooking. Timing is important to prevent overcooking and drying out.

Moist heat cookery includes braising, stewing, poaching and steaming. Here the chicken is usually browned, then liquid is added. The mixture is covered and cooked slowly to tenderize the meat. The less tender cuts are ideal here because they benefit from long, slow cooking.

Roasting a whole bird: Clean and stuff the chicken, if desired. Preheat the oven. Use a shallow ovenproof pan or dish that fits the bird. Place chicken on a rack in

BONING WINGS

Boned chicken wings can be stuffed with a variety of ingredients and are easier to eat than unboned wings. Smaller wings make excellent barbecued or pan-fried entrées. Use larger wings for main course dishes.

Using a small sharp knife and starting at the drum-stick end, slip knife down sides of bone towards the joint, without piercing the skin. Snap the bone free and proceed with the next joint in the same way, taking care not to pierce the elbow. Remove the bones and reshape the wing reading for stuffing

the pan and put a little wine or water in the bottom of the pan, if desired. Brush all over with melted butter or oil. If breast is browning too quickly, cover with a piece of foil. Cook according to directions in the recipe, basting occasionally. After roasting, let the bird rest for 10 minutes, covered loosely with foil, before carving.

Grilling or barbecuing: Give the grill plenty of time to heat up, so that the chicken is cooking over glowing coals rather than flames. To check the temperature of your fire, briefly hold your hand, palm down, about 5 inches above the coals, counting the seconds before you pull your hand away: 5 seconds - medium-low coals, 4 seconds - medium coals, 3 seconds - medium-hot coals, and 2 seconds - hot coals. Cooking times will depend on the thickness of the

chicken pieces and the temperature of the coals. There is a tendency for the outside of the chicken to cook too fast when the fire is too hot. If this happens, move the pieces further away from the heat, or brown the outside and then continue cooking wrapped in foil. (Serve wrapped in foil to preserve juices.) Brush unwrapped pieces with marinade, butter or oil during cooking to prevent drying out.

Broiling: Preheat the broiler and place chicken pieces on a cold, oiled broiler pan. Arrange pieces skin-side down and cook about 4–6-inches from the heat for about 15–20 minutes per side until the juices run clear and no pink remains near bone. Brush with marinade during cooking to prevent chicken drying out. If not using a marinade, chicken can be brushed with butter, herb butter

or oil during cooking. If skin is intact, brushing with oil or butter may not be necessary. The skin will help prevent drying out.

Stir-frying: This is the traditional Oriental or Asian way

To barbecue, place chicken on a preheated grill. Brush with marinade.

of cooking meat. This rapid method uses neatly cut strips of chicken, trimmed of fat. The strips must be evenly cut so that they cook at the same rate. Heat a little oil in a wok or large skillet and tilt the pan so that the bottom and sides are evenly coated. Stir-fry by tossing chicken quickly in small batches over high heat until cooked.

Pan-frying: This method is best for small, tender chicken pieces. Heat oil or butter in a skillet on high heat, add chicken pieces and cook for 2–3 minutes on each side to brown and seal in juices, turning with tongs. Reduce heat,

To roast, place on a rack in an oven tray. Brush with melted butter or oil.

Insert a skewer into thigh; if juice runs clear, the chicken is cooked.

To stir-fry, toss even-sized chicken pieces over high heat in wok or pan.

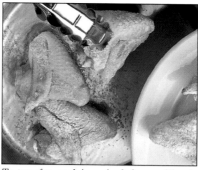

To pan-fry, cook in a single layer without crowding the pan.

To deep-fry, cook pieces in hot oil. When ready, remove and drain.

cover pan if necessary and cook as directed. Do not crowd the pan. Use a wide, heavy-based pan or two smaller pans so that the chicken will fit in a single layer rather than trying to fit too much into one pan. If the chicken is cooked without a coating, pat

pieces dry with paper towels before cooking.

Deep-frying: Preheat a deep saucepan or a deep-fat fryer with 1½–2-inches of vegetable oil. Heat to 365°F or test by dropping a square of dry bread into the hot oil. If the bread browns within

15 seconds and the oil bubbles and sizzles, it is hot enough for cooking. The chicken pieces should be of equal size so that they will cook at the same time. Follow individual recipe instructions for cooking method and timing.

Braising: This long, slow cooking process brings out the best in chicken, and will transform even an older bird into a delicious dish. The chicken should be gently simmered, never boiled, in the cooking liquid—boiling will make the chicken flesh tough. Brown whole birds or chicken pieces in butter or oil, then transfer to a casserole or baking dish, with vegetables and cooking liquids such as broth and wine. If cooked on top of the stove in a Dutch oven, the dish is covered, brought quickly to the boil, then the heat is reduced to a simmer. For oven cooking, cover the pot and cook at a temperature low enough to prevent the liquid from reaching a hard boil.

Poaching: In this method, the chicken is gently simmered in

CARVING

Let the cooked bird stand for 10 minutes in a warm place, covered loosely with foil. (This rests the meat and makes it easier to carve.) Place on a carving board or secure surface. Using a two-pronged fork to hold the bird and a sharp carving knife, cut around the leg, taking in a reasonable amount of flesh from the sides, first by cutting through the skin and then using the tip of the knife to separate the bone at the joint. Cut above the wing joint, through the breast bone. Separate legs by cutting into thigh and drumstick. Carve breast meat in slices parallel to the rib cage. Place pieces on a warm serving platter with vegetables or directly onto serving plates. Give each person some white and dark meat.

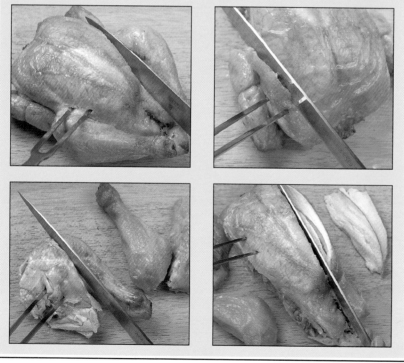

To casserole or braise, chicken is first browned quickly to seal in juices.

To poach, simmer chicken gently in wine or water until tender.

water, broth or wine, sometimes with vegetables and herbs added for flavor. The cooking liquid must never boil. This is a suitable method for cooking large chickens in a large kettle or Dutch oven or smaller chicken pieces in a shallow pan such as a skillet. After cooking, the liquid is strained and used to make a sauce to accompany the chicken or reserved for broth. Because of the low fat content, especially if skin is removed, poached chicken is ideal for dieters.

WINES TO SERVE WITH CHICKEN:

White wines are the perfect complement for chicken, with different wines for different dishes. White wines should be served well chilled. In hot weather, place the bottle of wine into an ice bucket or a wine cooler. Light, fresh fruity wines, such as sauvignon blanc are perfect with cold chicken. Stronger-flavored white wines that have more body, and matured wines, such as aged oaky chardonnays, gewurztraminer and rieslings, are well matched with savory, rich chicken dishes. Some lighter red wines can also be served with chicken. A chilled rosé is a great accompaniment to salads and cold dishes, while beaujolais-style wines are excellent with chicken burgers, pan-fried or barbecued chicken. Sparkling wines, such as dry champagnes, are excellent partners for delicious creamy chicken dishes.

CHICKEN STOCK

Many recipes in this book call for chicken stock. This is easy to prepare at home and imparts the best flavor to the dishes it is used in.

Chicken stock can be refrigerated or frozen in convenient amounts for up to 8 weeks. Fill ice cube trays with stock and freeze so that you can use a small amount for a sauce. For recipes that call for large amounts of stock, such as soups or stews, measure stock by the cup into plastic containers, label them and freeze.

Chicken bones for making stock can be purchased from butchers and specialty food stores. The neck and giblets removed from a whole roasting chicken can also be added for extra flavor.

If light chicken stock is specified in a recipe, dilute the basic stock with one-third water or until it reaches the desired strength.

Chicken stock can be purchased frozen from large supermarkets or health food stores. Canned chicken broth can be substituted. Chicken bouillon cubes or granules are also available.

CHICKEN STOCK
Makes 4 cups

1 lb chicken bones
1 large onion, chopped
2 bay leaves
6 peppercorns
1 carrot, chopped
1 stalk celery (leaves included), chopped
4–5 cups water

PREHEAT OVEN to moderate 350°F.
1 Place chicken bones and onion in a baking dish. Bake 50 minutes until well browned. Transfer bones and onion to large pan or stockpot.
2 Wrap bay leaves and peppercorns in a piece of cheesecloth to make a bouquet garni. Add with remaining ingredients to pan. Bring to a boil and reduce heat; simmer, uncovered, 40 minutes; add a little more water if necessary. Strain. Discard bones and vegetables. Cool quickly and refrigerate or freeze. After refrigeration, skim any hard fat that may have risen to the surface. Use stock as indicated in recipe.

TRADITIONAL CHICKEN GRAVY

This recipe makes enough delicious gravy to serve 4–6 people. White wine, marsala, chopped fresh herbs or mushrooms can be added. Store leftover gravy separate from chicken, in the refrigerator.

To make gravy: Sprinkle 2 tablespoons all-purpose flour evenly over a baking sheet. Place under a preheated broiler until flour is golden. Add to pan juices from roasting chicken, stir over low heat for 2 minutes. Add 3/4 cup of chicken stock to pan gradually, stirring until smooth. Stir constantly over medium heat for 5 minutes or until gravy boils and thickens; boil a further 1 minute and remove from heat. Pour into a warmed gravy boat and serve hot with chicken.

FAMILY FAVORITES

CHICKEN AND SPINACH LASAGNA

Preparation time: 30 minutes
Total cooking time: 1 hour 10 minutes
Serves 8

12 lasagna noodles
1 lb fresh spinach or 2 packages
 (10 oz each) frozen leaf
 spinach, thawed
1 tablespoon vegetable oil
2 lb ground raw chicken
1 clove garlic, finely chopped
3 slices bacon, chopped
1 can (14¹/2 oz) Italian-style
 tomatoes
2 cans (6 oz each) Italian-style
 tomato paste
1 can (8 oz) tomato sauce
²/3 cup chicken broth or stock
salt and pepper
1¹/2 cups grated cheddar cheese
 (for top)

Cheese Sauce
¹/4 cup butter or margarine
¹/2 cup all-purpose flour
3 cups milk
1¹/2 cups shredded cheddar
 cheese

PREHEAT OVEN to moderate 375°F. Grease a 9 x 13 x 2-inch baking dish. Cook lasagna following package directions until firm but tender. Drain. Rinse with cold water; drain again.

1 Remove stems from fresh spinach; discard. In a large saucepan, bring water to boil. Add spinach leaves; cook 1–2 minutes or until tender. Drain well. If using frozen, thawed spinach, squeeze dry and set aside. Heat oil in a large skillet over medium heat; add chicken, garlic and bacon. Sauté 5 minutes or until well browned. Drain fat. Stir in undrained tomatoes, tomato paste, sauce, broth and salt and pepper to taste. Bring to a boil; reduce heat and simmer 10 minutes or until sauce is slightly thickened.

2 To make Cheese Sauce: Melt butter in a medium saucepan. Stir in flour. Gradually whisk in milk. Bring to a boil, stirring frequently; cook 1 minute. Stir in 1¹/2 cups cheese until melted. Remove from heat.

3 To assemble lasagna: Spread one-third of the chicken mixture into prepared pan. Top with four lasagna noodles. Spread with one-third of the cheese sauce, then one-third of the chicken mixture. Top with all the spinach, four lasagna noodles, one-third of the cheese sauce and the remaining chicken mixture. Arrange remaining lasagne noodles over chicken mixture. Spread evenly with remaining cheese sauce; sprinkle with remaining cheese. Bake 50 minutes or until cooked through and golden.

CHICKEN AND VEGETABLE HOT POT

Preparation time: 20 minutes
Total cooking time: 45 minutes
Serves 4

8 boneless, skinned chicken
    thighs (about 3 lb)
1/2 cup unsifted all-purpose flour
freshly ground black pepper,
    to taste
2 tablespoons vegetable oil
1 medium onion, sliced
1 clove garlic, finely chopped
4 slices bacon, chopped
2 medium potatoes, peeled and
    cut into 3/4–inch cubes
1 large carrot, sliced

1 celery stalk, sliced
2 medium zucchini, sliced
2 cups cauliflower florets
1 can (14 1/2 oz) crushed tomatoes
3 tablespoons tomato paste
3/4 cup dry red wine
3/4 cup chicken broth or stock
salt and pepper

TRIM CHICKEN thighs of excess fat
and sinew

1 Combine the flour and black
pepper. Toss the chicken lightly in the
seasoned flour and shake off excess.
In a large skillet, heat the oil. Cook
chicken over medium heat, turning
occasionally, until browned, cooked
through, and no longer pink near the
bone (about 20 minutes). Drain on
paper towels; keep warm.

2 Add the sliced onion, garlic and
bacon to the skillet. Cook and stir over
medium-high heat, until the onion is
tender. Drain fat. Add the potatoes,
carrot and celery; cook, stirring, for
about 2 minutes. Add the zucchini,
cauliflower, undrained crushed
tomatoes, tomato paste, wine and
broth. Season to taste.

3 Bring to a boil; reduce heat.
Simmer, covered, 10–15 minutes,
stirring occasionally, or until the
vegetables are tender. Do not
overcook. Add the chicken to sauce
mixture. Cook, uncovered, for
5 minutes or until heated through.

COOK'S FILE

Storage time: Cook this dish just
before serving.

LEMON CHICKEN

Preparation time: 15 minutes
Total cooking time: 1 hour 15 minutes
Serves 4

1 x 2¹/₂–3 lb whole broiler-fryer
1 tablespoon soy sauce
1 tablespoon dry sherry
1 tablespoon lemon juice
2 teaspoons brown sugar

Lemon Sauce
2 green onions, thinly sliced
¹/₂ cup lemon juice
¹/₂ cup sugar
2 teaspoons dry sherry
1 teaspoon soy sauce
1 tablespoon cornstarch
¹/₂ cup water
salt and white pepper

PREHEAT OVEN to 350°F.
1 Remove giblets and any large deposits of fat from the chicken. Rinse and pat dry with paper towels. Tie wings and drumsticks securely in place. Place chicken, breast-side up, on a rack in a roasting pan. Combine soy sauce, sherry, lemon juice and brown sugar. Brush chicken with the soy mixture.
2 Roast the chicken for about 1¹/₂ –2 hours or until the juices run clear and the meat thermometer inserted into thigh meat reaches 180°F internal temperature. Baste the chicken occasionally with the remaining soy mixture. Remove from oven and let stand, covered with foil, for about 10 minutes before carving. Serve chicken hot with Lemon Sauce and steamed rice or noodles.
3 While chicken is in oven, cut green onions into long thin strips; place in iced water until curly.
4 To make Lemon Sauce: in small saucepan, combine lemon juice, sugar, sherry and soy sauce. Combine cornstarch and water in small bowl; add to pan. Stir over medium heat 4 minutes or until sauce boils and thickens slightly. Season to taste; stir in green onions.

COOK'S FILE

Variation: Chicken breast fillets can be used in this recipe. Cut into strips, combine with soy mixture and drain. Stir-fry until cooked but not browned. Combine with Lemon Sauce and serve.

1

2

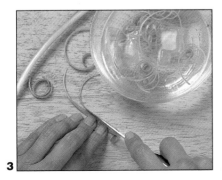

3

4

CHICKEN AND MACARONI BAKE

Preparation time: 20 minutes
Total cooking time: 55 minutes
Serves 6

1 lb boneless, skinned chicken
   breasts
3 cups elbow macaroni
2 tablespoons olive oil
1 medium onion, chopped
1 medium carrot,
   chopped
4 slices bacon, chopped
2 medium zucchini, chopped
1 can (10¾ oz) tomato soup
1 cup sour cream
salt and pepper
2 cups shredded cheddar
   cheese

TRIM CHICKEN of excess fat and sinew. Preheat oven to 375°F. Cook macaroni according to package directions until firm but tender. Drain; rinse with cold water; drain again.

1 Cut chicken into ¾-inch cubes. In large saucepan, heat oil. Cook chicken over medium-high heat until browned and cooked through, about 5 minutes; drain on paper towels.

2 Add onion, carrot and bacon to pan. Cook over medium heat 10 minutes; stir occasionally. Add zucchini and soup. Bring to a boil; simmer, covered, for 5 minutes. Remove from heat.

3 Combine the cooked pasta, chicken, tomato mixture, and sour cream. Season with salt and pepper. Spread in a 9 x 13 x 2-inch baking dish or a shallow 3-quart casserole dish. Top with cheese. Bake 20–25 minutes or until golden and heated through.

1

2

3

COUNTRY-FRIED CHICKEN

Preparation time: 10 minutes
Total cooking time: 25 minutes
Serves 6

12 chicken drumsticks
1/3 cup crushed cornflakes
1 1/2 cups unsifted all-purpose
    flour
2 tablespoons instant chicken
    bouillon powder
1 teaspoon celery salt
1 teaspoon onion salt
1/2 teaspoon garlic powder
1/2 teaspoon ground white
    pepper
oil for deep frying

1 Place chicken in large pan of boiling water; return to a boil. Reduce heat; simmer, uncovered, 15 minutes or until chicken is cooked through. Lift out with tongs; drain.

2 In a medium bowl, combine the cornflake crumbs and flour, bouillon powder, celery salt and onion salt. Place the drumsticks into a large bowl and cover with cold water. Dip the wet drumsticks, one at a time, into the seasoned flour mixture and shake off the excess.

3 In a large saucepan or fryer, heat 1 1/2 inches of oil. Gently lower the chicken drumsticks, 1 or 2 pieces at a time, into moderately hot oil (365°F). Cook for about 8 minutes or until golden brown. Carefully remove chicken from oil with tongs or slotted spoon. Drain on paper towels; keep warm. Repeat with remaining chicken pieces. Serve hot.

COOK'S FILE

Hint: Pre-cooking the chicken before frying ensures that it will be cooked through without the skin burning.

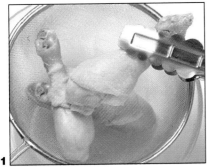

CHICKEN AND HAM PIE

Preparation time: 35 minutes
Total cooking time: 1 hour
Serves 6

refrigerated shortcrust pastry
    for single crust (1/2 a 15-oz
    package) or 71/2 oz home-
    made shortcrust pastry
1 lb boneless, skinned chicken
    thighs, cut in 3/4–inch pieces
1 tablespoon vegetable oil
1/4 cup butter or margarine
1 medium onion, chopped
1/3 cup unsifted all-purpose flour
11/3 cups milk
11/4 cups shredded cheddar
    cheese
1 tablespoon prepared mustard
1 cup chopped ham
1/2 sweet red pepper, chopped
3 green onions, chopped
2 hard-boiled eggs, quartered
1 sheet frozen puff pastry
1 large egg, beaten

PREHEAT OVEN to 400°F. Brush a
10-inch quiche pan with melted butter
or oil.

1 If using home-made pastry, roll out
on a lightly floured surface, large
enough to cover base and sides of
prepared pan.

2 Line the quiche pan with pastry
(follow package directions for ready-
made pastry) and line the bottom of
crust with heavy-duty foil. Spread a
layer of dried beans evenly over the
foil. Bake for 7 minutes. Carefully
remove the foil and beans; bake for
8 minutes more or until pastry is
golden brown. Cool. Reduce oven
temperature to 350°F.

3 Trim the chicken of any excess fat
and sinew. In a large skillet, heat the
oil. Add the chicken and cook over
medium-high heat until cooked
through, about 10 minutes. Drain on
paper towels.

4 Add the butter to the pan and heat
gently. Add the chopped onion and
cook until tender. Stir in the flour.
Gradually whisk in the milk, stirring
until smooth. Bring the mixture to
boil, stirring frequently. Cook for
1 minute. Add the shredded cheddar
cheese and stir until melted. Remove
pan from the heat. Stir in the mustard,
ham, red pepper, green onion and
cooked chicken.

5 Spoon half the mixture into the
prepared pastry crust. Top with the
hard-cooked egg wedges and then top
with the remaining chicken mixture.

6 Trim the puff pastry to fit the
quiche dish and place on top of the
mixture, sealing the edge with some of
the beaten egg. Brush top of pastry
with beaten egg. Make a few slashes
in top crust to allow steam to escape.
If desired, decorate with trimmings of
puff pastry. Bake pie for about
40–45 minutes or until pastry is
golden. Serve hot.

COOK'S FILE

Storage time: Chicken and Ham Pie
can be assembled one day ahead up to
the final baking. Store the pie, covered
with plastic wrap, in the refrigerator.
Remove pie from the refrigerator,
bake in preheated oven for 45 minutes
as directed, then serve.

Variation: Leftover cooked chicken
can be used instead of the thigh fillets.
Cut or shred into 3/4–inch pieces and
use as directed.
You can also make individual chicken
and ham pies or substitute puff pastry
for the shortcrust and make individual
chicken and ham turnovers.

Hint: Accompanied by a dollop of
sour cream, a sprig of a fresh herb
and a warmed bread roll, this pie
becomes a dress-up lunch dish. Serve
with a chilled white wine.

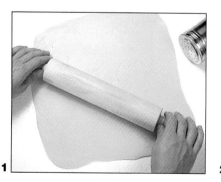

1

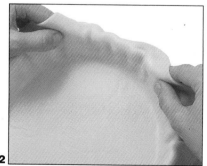

2

3

4

5

6

CHICKEN AND TOMATO RISOTTO

Preparation time: 15 minutes
Total cooking time: 40 minutes
Serves 4

2 lb meaty chicken pieces
2 tablespoons olive oil
2 large onions, chopped
2 large carrots, quartered
   lengthwise and cut into
   1/4–inch pieces
1 cup short-grain rice

2 single-serving-size envelopes
   (1 oz each) instant tomato
   soup mix
3 cups chicken broth or stock
1/4 teaspoon ground black
   pepper
1/4 cup chopped fresh cilantro

REMOVE THE skin from chicken, if desired.

1 In a large skillet, heat the oil over medium-high heat. Add the chicken; cook about 10 minutes, turning frequently, until golden brown. Remove from pan; drain on paper towels.

2 Add onion and carrot to pan; stir over medium heat 5 minutes or until golden. Add rice and stir over low heat for 5 minutes.

3 Combine tomato soup mix, broth and pepper; add to pan. Stir until mixture boils. Return chicken to pan, reduce heat. Simmer, covered, for 20 minutes or until the chicken is tender, rice cooked and liquid absorbed. Stir in cilantro. Serve hot.

COOK'S FILE

Storage time: Cook this dish just before serving.

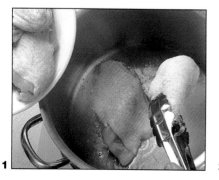

CHICKEN WITH TARRAGON AND MUSHROOMS

Preparation time: 10 minutes
Total cooking time: 45 minutes
Serves 6

2 tablespoons olive oil
6 large (1 1/2 lb) boneless, skinned chicken breast halves
3 slices thick-sliced bacon, cut in 1/4–inch pieces (or 2 oz Canadian bacon, cut in strips)

8 oz fresh mushrooms, thinly sliced
1/2 cup dry white wine
3 tablespoons tomato paste
1 teaspoon dried tarragon
2/3 cup heavy cream
3 green onions, finely chopped
salt and pepper

PREHEAT THE oven to 350°F.

1 In a large skillet, heat the olive oil. Add the chicken. Cook over medium-high heat for about 2 minutes each side, turning once, just until browned. Remove chicken from the pan and drain on paper towels. Place chicken in a shallow baking dish; set aside.

2 Add the bacon to the pan and cook over medium-high heat for 2 minutes; drain the fat. Add the mushrooms and cook for 5 minutes. Add the wine, tomato paste and tarragon to the pan; stir until the mixture boils. Reduce the heat and add the cream; simmer for 2 minutes. Remove pan from the heat and stir in the green onions. Season to taste with salt and pepper.

3 Pour the sauce over the chicken. Bake, covered, for 20–30 minutes or until the chicken is tender.

1

2

3

SAVORY CHICKEN LOAF

Preparation time: 30 minutes +
  15 minutes refrigeration
Total cooking time: 1 hour 5 minutes
Serves 4 to 6

Crust
2 tablespoons butter or
  margarine, melted
3 cups unsifted all-purpose flour
1¹/2 teaspoons baking powder
¹/2 teaspoon salt
¹/3 cup butter or margarine,
  cut into pieces
³/4 cup cold water

Filling
1 tablespoon olive oil
1 lb ground raw chicken
3 slices bacon, chopped
1 package (10 oz) frozen
  chopped spinach, thawed and
  squeezed dry
1 large tomato, peeled, seeded
  and chopped
1¹/4 cups shredded cheddar cheese
3 tablespoons all-purpose flour

¹/4 teaspoon ground cayenne
  pepper
1 large egg, beaten
¹/3 cup chopped fresh parsley
salt and pepper

PREHEAT OVEN to 375°F. Brush a
5 x 9 x 3-inch loaf pan with half of the
melted butter; set aside.

1 For crust, in a food processor bowl,
combine flour, baking powder, salt,
and chopped butter. Using pulse action,
process 20 seconds or until fine and
crumbly. Add water a little at a time;
process 15 seconds or until soft dough
forms. (If desired, combine crust
ingredients in a large bowl. With pastry
blender, cut butter into flour mixture
until fine and crumbly. Gradually add
water and mix until soft dough forms.)

2 Turn dough onto a lightly floured
surface. Roll three-quarters of dough
into a rectangle, cover bottom and
sides of loaf pan and extend slightly
over edges. Roll remaining dough into a
10 x 6-inch rectangle. Cover both with
plastic wrap; refrigerate.

3 To make Filling: Heat oil in a
large skillet or saucepan. Sauté chicken
and bacon over medium-high heat, until
browned; break up any large pieces of
chicken. Remove from heat. Drain fat;
Stir in spinach, tomato, cheese, flour,
cayenne pepper, egg, parsley and salt
and pepper to taste. Mix well.

4 Spoon into loaf pan. Top with
remaining dough; pinch edges to seal.
Cut 2 or 3 small slits in the top to allow
steam to escape. Brush with remaining
melted butter. Bake for 40–50 minutes
or until browned and cooked through.
Leave loaf 15 minutes before removing
from pan. Serve sliced, hot or cold.

MUSHROOM-STUFFED CHICKEN WITH HERB BUTTER

Preparation time: 20 minutes +
  10 minutes standing
Total cooking time: 2 hours 25 minutes
Serves 6

2 tablespoons olive oil
1 large onion, finely chopped
2 cups finely chopped
  mushrooms
1/3 cup chopped sun-dried
  tomatoes
1/3 cup short-grain rice
1 tablespoon tomato paste
1 cup chicken broth or stock
1/2 cup peeled and coarsely
  grated apple
1 whole (2 1/2–3 lb) broiler-fryer
  chicken

freshly cracked black pepper
2 tablespoons butter or
  margarine, melted

Herb Butter
1/3 cup butter or margarine,
  softened
1 tablespoon tomato paste
2 teaspoons dried Italian herbs,
  crushed
1/2 teaspoon cracked black
  peppercorns or freshly
  ground pepper

PREHEAT OVEN to 350°F.

1 In a large skillet or saucepan, heat oil. Add onion; stir over medium heat for 5 minutes or until tender. Add mushrooms, cook on medium-high heat 7 minutes or until well browned. Add sun-dried tomatoes, rice, tomato paste and chicken broth; bring to boil. Reduce heat; simmer, covered, for 15 minutes. Remove from heat; stir in the grated apple.

2 Remove neck and giblets from chicken. Rinse and pat dry with paper towels. Spoon stuffing into chicken cavity; close cavity and secure with a toothpick or skewer. Tie wings and drumsticks in place with string. Brush chicken with butter; coat all over with freshly cracked black pepper. Place the chicken, breast-side up on rack in a roasting pan. Roast for 1 1/2–2 hours until thermometer inserted into thigh meat registers 180°F. Remove chicken from the oven and let stand, covered loosely with foil, for 10 minutes before carving. Serve hot, accompanied with Herb Butter.

3 **To make Herb Butter:** In a small mixing bowl, beat the butter, tomato paste, Italian herbs and peppercorns with a wooden spoon until light and creamy.

ROAST CHICKEN WITH BREAD CRUMB STUFFING

Preparation time: 25 minutes +
　10 minutes standing
Total cooking time: 2 hours 10 minutes
Serves 4 to 6

3 slices thick-sliced bacon,
　finely chopped
4 cups (about 6 slices bread)
　whole wheat bread cubes
3 green onions, chopped
3 tablespoons chopped pecans
1 tablespoon dried currants
1/3 cup finely chopped parsley
1/3 cup milk
1 large egg, beaten
salt and pepper
1 whole broiler-fryer chicken
　(2 1/2–3 lb)
freshly ground black pepper
3 tablespoons butter or
　margarine, melted
1 tablespoon vegetable oil
1 tablespoon soy sauce
1 1/2 cups water
1 clove garlic, crushed
2 tablespoons unsifted
　all-purpose flour

PREHEAT OVEN to 350°F.

1 In a skillet, cook bacon over high heat 5 minutes or until crisp. Drain on paper towels. In a large bowl, combine bacon, bread cubes, onion, pecans, currants and parsley. Combine egg and milk; add to mixture. Season to taste with salt and pepper; mix well.

2 Remove neck, giblets and any fat from chicken. Rinse well and pat dry with paper towels. Spoon stuffing into chicken cavity; close cavity and secure with a skewer or toothpick. Tie wings and drumsticks securely in place with string. Rub chicken all over with salt and freshly ground black pepper.

3 Place chicken, breast-side up, on rack in a roasting pan. Combine butter, oil and soy sauce. Brush chicken with butter mixture. Pour any leftover mixture into roasting pan along with half the water and garlic. Roast chicken 1 1/2–2 hours or until browned and thermometer inserted into thigh meat registers 180°F. Brush occasionally with pan juices during cooking. Transfer to a serving platter. Let stand, loosely covered with foil, for 10 minutes before carving. Serve with gravy and vegetables.

5 To make gravy, strain pan juices into a medium saucepan. Combine flour and remaining water until smooth. Add flour mixture to pan juices. Stir constantly over medium heat 5 minutes or until mixture boils and thickens. Season to taste. (Add extra water if necessary.) Serve hot.

COOK'S FILE

Hint: Substitute white wine for half the water in gravy, if desired.

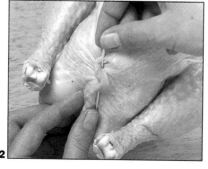

1

3

PINEAPPLE AND PEPPER CHICKEN WINGS

Preparation time: 10 minutes
Total cooking time: 35 minutes
Serves 4

12 small chicken wings
    (about 2–2¹/₂ lb)
3 tablespoons cornstarch
¹/₂ teaspoon ground ginger
1 teaspoon onion salt
2 tablespoons vegetable oil
1 medium onion, cut in thin wedges
2 medium sweet red peppers,
    cut in long thin strips

1 can (15¹/₄ oz) pineapple
    tidbits in light syrup
1 teaspoon instant chicken
    bouillon powder
1 tablespoon soy sauce
1 tablespoon barbecue sauce

PREHEAT OVEN to 350°F. Tuck chicken wing tips to the underside. Combine cornstarch, ginger and onion salt in large bowl. Add chicken; toss to coat. Shake off excess.

1 In large skillet, heat oil. Add chicken. Cook over medium-high heat for 5 minutes, turning occasionally, until browned. Remove from pan and drain on paper towels.

2 Add onion and red pepper to skillet (add more oil if necessary). Stir over medium heat 5 minutes. Stir in undrained pineapple, chicken bouillon, soy sauce and barbecue sauce. Bring to boil; remove from heat.

3 Arrange chicken in a single layer in a shallow baking dish. Pour pepper mixture over chicken. Bake, uncovered, 25 minutes or until chicken is cooked through; turn chicken once during cooking. Serve immediately with steamed rice, if desired.

COOK'S FILE

Storage time: Cook this dish just before serving

GREEN CHICKEN CURRY

Preparation time: 10 minutes
Total cooking time: 40 minutes
Serves 4

8 chicken thigh cutlets
    (about 2¹/₂–3 lb)
2 tablespoons peanut oil
3 cloves garlic, finely chopped
1 tablespoon grated fresh ginger
3 green onions, finely chopped
1 teaspoon curry powder
¹/₄ cup chopped green chili
    peppers
¹/₂ teaspoon ground coriander
¹/₂ teaspoon ground cumin
1¹/₄ cups water

²/₃ cup canned coconut milk
²/₃ cup chopped fresh cilantro
1 tablespoon Thai fish sauce
    (nam pla)
2 medium tomatoes, seeded and
    chopped

TRIM CHICKEN of excess fat and sinew, removing skin, if desired.

1 In large skillet over medium-high heat, heat oil. Add garlic, ginger, green onions and curry powder. Cook, stirring, for 1 minute. Stir in the chili peppers, coriander and cumin.

2 Add chicken. Cook over medium heat 5 minutes; turn once. Carefully add water; cover. Simmer 15 minutes.

3 Stir in the coconut milk, cilantro, fish sauce and chopped tomatoes.

Simmer, uncovered, for 10–15 minutes more or until the chicken is tender and cooked through. Serve Green Chicken Curry with hot steamed or boiled rice, if desired.

COOK'S FILE

Storage time: This dish can be made one day ahead. Store, covered, in the refrigerator.

Hints: Soy sauce can be substituted for the fish sauce. However, for an authentic Thai flavor, fish sauce should be used. It is readily available at most supermarkets or from Oriental food stores.

Note: Do not cover the pan after adding coconut cream to a dish as it may separate.

Pineapple and Pepper Chicken Wings (top)
and Green Chicken Curry

CHICKEN PAPRIKA WITH HERB DUMPLINGS

Preparation time: 20 minutes
Total cooking time: 1 hour 10 minutes
Serves 4 to 6

1 broiler-fryer chicken, cut up
    (about 2½–3 lb)
2 tablespoons vegetable oil
1 large onion, chopped
1 clove garlic, finely chopped
1 can (14½ oz) crushed
    tomatoes
1 teaspoon paprika
1 teaspoon dried thyme, crushed
3 tablespoons unsifted
    all-purpose flour
½ cup chicken broth or stock
Salt and pepper
2 medium carrots, sliced

Herb Dumplings
1 cup unsifted all-purpose flour
1½ teaspoons baking powder
¼ teaspoon baking soda
¼ teaspoon salt
2 tablespoons butter or
    margarine, cut into pieces
2 teaspoons finely chopped
    fresh parsley
2 teaspoons finely chopped
    fresh chives
½ teaspoon dried mixed herbs,
    crushed
⅓ cup buttermilk

PREHEAT OVEN to 350°F. Remove large deposits of fat from chicken. Remove skin, if desired. Rinse chicken and pat dry with paper towels.

1 In a large skillet, heat oil. Cook the chicken pieces over medium-high heat until browned, about 10 minutes. Place browned chicken in a 3-quart deep casserole or baking dish. Add onion and garlic to skillet; cook over medium heat until onion is tender. Add tomatoes, paprika and thyme. Combine flour and chicken broth until smooth; add to mixture. Cook, stirring, 2–3 minutes until slightly thickened. Season to taste. Pour mixture over chicken. Place carrots around chicken. Cover and bake for 30 minutes.

2 To make Herb Dumplings: In a medium mixing bowl, combine flour, baking powder, soda, salt and butter. Using fingertips or a pastry blender, rub or cut butter into flour mixture until fine and crumbly. Stir in parsley, chives and herbs. Add buttermilk; mix to a soft dough. (Add 1 tablespoon additional buttermilk, if necessary.)

3 Turn onto a floured surface and knead for 1 minute or until smooth. Divide dough into eight equal portions, and form into rough balls.

4 Remove the casserole from the oven and arrange dumplings on the top. Bake, uncovered, 20 minutes longer, until dumplings are brown. Serve immediately.

CHICKEN PAELLA

Preparation time: 10 minutes
Total cooking time: 45 minutes
Serves 4

8 chicken drumsticks
   (about 2–2¹/2 lb)
2 tablespoons olive oil
1 oz pepperoni sausage, thinly
   sliced
1 large onion, cut in thin
   wedges
2 cloves garlic, crushed
1 teaspoon turmeric
1 cup short-grain rice
2 cups chicken broth or stock

1 medium sweet red pepper, cut
   into short, thin strips
9–10 oz fresh or frozen, cut
   green beans
1 cup small broccoli florets
   (about 4 oz)
salt and pepper
8 medium fresh shrimp, peeled
   and deveined (6–8 oz)

TRIM CHICKEN of excess fat; remove skin, if desired.

1 Heat the oil in a large heavy-based saucepan. Cook the chicken a few pieces at a time, over medium-high heat for 10–15 minutes, until well browned. Remove from the pan; drain. Fry the sausage for 1 minute; add onion and garlic to pan and cook, stirring, for 1 minute.

2 Add the turmeric and rice to the pan; cook for 1 minute until rice is coated with oil. Add the broth, pepper, beans and broccoli; season to taste. Bring to a boil; reduce heat to low.

3 Place chicken on rice. Simmer, covered, 15 minutes. Add shrimp; cover and cook 10–15 minutes more or until liquid is absorbed and chicken and rice are tender. Serve hot.

COOK'S FILE

Hint: Paella is traditionally cooked and served in a pan called a 'paellera'. If you plan to cook it often, it is definitely worth buying a paellera.

CRISPY TOMATO AND ONION CHICKEN

Preparation time: 20 minutes
Total cooking time: 45 minutes
Serves 4 to 6

1 broiler-fryer chicken
   (about 2¹/₂–3 lb),
   cut up
1 envelope (1¹/₄ oz) dry onion
   soup mix

2 envelopes (1 oz each) instant
   tomato soup mix
2 medium onions
2 medium carrots
2 medium zucchini
freshly ground black pepper

PREHEAT OVEN to 400°F. Trim chicken of excess fat. Remove skin, if desired. Rinse chicken and pat dry with paper towels.

1 In a bowl or plastic bag, combine soup mixes. Coat chicken pieces with soup mixture. Shake off excess.

2 Chop onions, carrots and zucchini. Place in a single layer in a 9 x 13-inch baking pan. Add pepper to taste.

3 Place chicken pieces on top of vegetables. Bake, uncovered, for 40–45 minutes or until chicken is browned and no longer pink near bone.

COOK'S FILE

For a flavor change, add 1 teaspoon each of ground cumin, paprika and garlic powder to soup mixtures.

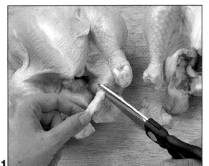

ROAST CHICKEN WITH BACON AND SAGE STUFFING

Preparation time: 15 minutes
Total cooking time: 1 hour 15 minutes
  to 1 hour 35 minutes
Serves 6

2 broiler-fryer chickens
    (about 2–2¹/2 lb each)
2 slices thick-sliced bacon,
    chopped
1 medium onion, finely
    chopped
1 tablespoon chopped fresh sage
    or ¹/2 teaspoon dried sage
2 cups soft bread crumbs
1 large egg, beaten
salt and pepper
1 tablespoon vegetable oil
2 slices thick-sliced bacon, cut
    lengthwise into strips

PREHEAT OVEN to moderate 375°F.
1 Remove neck, giblets and any large fat deposits from chicken. Rinse chicken and dry with paper towels.
2 In a large skillet, cook bacon and onion until bacon is brown and onion is tender. Drain. Transfer to a mixing bowl; cool. Add sage, bread crumbs and egg; mix well and season to taste.
3 Spoon stuffing into chicken cavities; close with skin; secure with a skewer or toothpick. Fold wing tips underneath; tie legs together to keep in place. Place chickens, breast-side up, in a large roasting pan. Brush with oil.

4 Place strips of bacon across chicken breasts. Bake for 1¹/4–1¹/2 hours, or until thermometer inserted into thigh meat registers 180°F. Let stand for about 10 minutes before carving. Serve chicken immediately with seasonal vegetables.

COOK'S FILE

Storage time: Cook this dish just before serving. The stuffing can be made up to 2 hours ahead. Store, covered, in the refrigerator. Stuff chickens immediately before baking.

APRICOT CHICKEN

Preparation time: 15 minutes
Total cooking time: 30 minutes
Serves 6

3 lb boneless, skinned chicken
   thigh meat
1 tablespoon vegetable oil
1 cup dried apricots, cut into
   strips
1½ cups apricot nectar
⅔ cup chicken broth or stock
1 envelope (1¼ oz) dried onion
   soup mix
1 tablespoon finely chopped
   fresh parsley

TRIM CHICKEN of any excess fat
and sinew.

1 Cut the chicken into 1-inch pieces.
In a large skillet, heat the oil. Cook the
chicken, in two batches, over medium-
high heat until browned; drain fat.

2 Add the apricot strips, apricot
nectar, broth and soup mix; stir
thoroughly to combine. Bring mixture
to a boil, reduce the heat and simmer,
covered, for 10 minutes. Uncover, and
cook 5–10 minutes more, stirring
occasionally until chicken is tender
and the sauce is slightly thickened.

3 Remove pan from heat. Stir in
parsley. Serve hot with steamed green
vegetables and crusty bread.

COOK'S FILE

Storage time: Apricot Chicken can
be made up to two days ahead. Cool
quickly and refrigerate until ready to
serve. Reheat gently.

Variations: Replace the dried
apricots and apricot nectar with a
large can of apricots with syrup, if
desired. Any cut of chicken can be
used in this recipe. Increase cooking
times for larger bone-in pieces.

1

2

3

CHICKEN CACCIATORE

Preparation time: 15 minutes
Total cooking time: 55 minutes
Serves 6

1 1/2 cups fresh mushrooms
1 medium onion
2 tablespoons vegetable oil
12 chicken drumsticks
    (about 3 lb)
1 clove garlic, crushed
1 can (14 1/2 oz) crushed
    tomatoes

2/3 cup chicken broth or stock
2/3 cup dry white wine
1 teaspoon dried oregano,
    crushed
1 teaspoon dried thyme, crushed
salt and pepper

PREHEAT OVEN to 350°F.
1 Cut the mushrooms into quarters and finely chop the onion.
2 In a large skillet, heat oil. Cook drumsticks, a few at a time, over medium-high heat until well browned, 10–15 minutes; transfer to a large ovenproof casserole dish.

3 Add onion and garlic to skillet; cook over medium heat until golden. Add the tomatoes, broth, white wine, mushrooms, oregano and thyme to skillet. Season to taste. Bring to a boil; reduce the heat and simmer for 10 minutes. Pour over the chicken. Bake, covered, 35–40 minutes or until chicken is very tender. Serve Chicken Cacciatore with hot spiral or other small pasta.

COOK'S FILE

Storage time: This dish can be made up to 2 days ahead.

BARBECUES AND GRILLS

CHICKEN BURGERS WITH BROWN MUSTARD CREAM

Preparation time: 12 minutes +
   20 minutes chilling
Total cooking time: 15 minutes
Makes 6

1/2 cup fine dry bread crumbs
1 tablespoon curry powder
3 tablespoons mango chutney
3 tablespoons finely chopped
   Italian parsley
1 large egg, beaten
salt and freshly ground black
   pepper, to taste
1¼ lb ground raw chicken

Brown Mustard Cream
1/3 cup sour cream
1 tablespoon brown mustard
1 tablespoon mango chutney,
   chopped
1/4 cup olive oil

6 split Kaiser rolls or
   hamburger buns, (optional)
   to serve

COMBINE BREAD CRUMBS, curry powder, chutney, parsley, egg, salt and pepper in a large bowl.

1 Add the chicken; press the mixture together with hands until combined.

2 Shape the mixture into 6 patties Cover patties with plastic wrap and chill for about 20 minutes. Meanwhile, prepare grill. To grill burgers, place on grid 5-inches above medium coals. Grill, uncovered, for 10–15 minutes or until no pink remains. Turn burgers halfway through the cooking time.

3 To make Brown Mustard Cream: In medium bowl, combine the sour cream, mustard and chutney. Using a wire whisk, stir to combine. Add the oil a little at a time; beat well after each addition, until all the oil has been added and mixture is fluffy. Serve burgers on split rolls or buns with Mustard Cream. Garnish with strips of roasted red pepper, if desired.

COOK'S FILE

Storage time: Uncooked patties can be frozen for up to four weeks. Stack patties, place two layers of plastic wrap between each and seal in an airtight container.

Hint: For a casual lunch, offer split and toasted rolls or buns, red onion rings, torn lettuce leaves, sliced tomatoes and any other ingredients you like. Let guests make their own burgers. Serve Brown Mustard Cream in a separate bowl.

Variation: You can add a tang to this recipe by using a hot curry paste instead of powder, or by adding cayenne pepper to taste.

BACON-WRAPPED CHICKEN

Preparation time: 15 minutes
Total cooking time: 30 minutes
Serves 3

2 tablespoons olive oil
2 tablespoons lime juice
1/4 teaspoon ground coriander
salt and pepper
1/3 cup chutney, chopped
1/4 cup finely chopped pecans

6 medium (about 1 1/4 lb)
  boneless, skinned chicken
  breast halves
6 slices bacon

PREPARE GRILL. Place oil, lime juice, coriander, salt and pepper in small bowl and mix well; set aside.

1 Using a sharp knife, cut a pocket along the side, in thickest part of each breast half. Combine chutney and nuts in a small bowl. Spoon 1 tablespoon of mixture into each breast pocket. Turn tapered end of breast to underside.

2 Wrap a bacon slice around each chicken breast half to hold the tapered ends in place and secure the bacon with a toothpick.

3 To grill, place the chicken pieces onto the center of grill. Cover the grill and cook over medium coals for about 10–15 minutes, until well browned and cooked through, turning once. Brush the chicken with the lime juice mixture several times during cooking.

COOK'S FILE

Storage time: Cook this dish just before serving. Chicken breasts can be assembled up to 2 hours beforehand. Cover and chill in refrigerator until ready to grill.

CRUNCHY HERB AND PARMESAN CHICKEN

Preparation time: 20 minutes
Total cooking time: 21 minutes
Serves 4

1/4 cup butter or margarine
1 tablespoon finely chopped chives
1 tablespoon finely chopped
    fresh basil
1 tablespoon finely chopped
    fresh mint
1 tablespoon finely chopped
    fresh dill
1 teaspoon finely grated lemon
    rind

2 teaspoons lemon juice
3 tablespoons grated Parmesan
    cheese
salt and pepper
8 chicken thighs (about 1 1/2 lb)
3 tablespoons grated Parmesan
    cheese, extra

LINE A BROILER pan with foil, place rack in pan. Brush rack with a little melted butter. Preheat broiler.
1 Using an electric beater, beat the butter until light and creamy. Add the herbs, lemon rind, lemon juice and the Parmesan cheese; beat mixture until well combined.
2 Loosen the skin from one end of each thigh. Spread herb butter underneath skin of each thigh. Secure skin to flesh with toothpicks.
3 Place thighs on prepared broiler pan, skin-side up; broil 6 inches from heat for 8–10 minutes. Turn chicken pieces over; broil 8–10 minutes longer or until chicken is no longer pink near bone. Turn chicken over with skin-side upon the pan; sprinkle with remaining Parmesan cheese and broil 1 minute more or until cheese is lightly browned. Discard toothpicks. Serve immediately.

COOK'S FILE

Chicken can be prepared up to Step 3, a day ahead. Refrigerate until ready to use. Broil just before serving.

TANDOORI CHICKEN ON SKEWERS

Preparation time: 15 minutes +
   3 hours marinating
Total cooking time: 10 minutes
Makes about 16

6 boneless, skinned chicken
   breast halves (about 1½ lb)
2 teaspoons turmeric
1 teaspoon sweet paprika
1 teaspoon garam masala
½ teaspoon ground cardamom
1 teaspoon ground coriander
1 small onion, grated

1 clove garlic, crushed
2 teaspoons lemon juice
2 teaspoons sugar
salt, to taste
1 carton (8 oz) plain yogurt
red food coloring (optional)
16 (10–inch) skewers

TRIM CHICKEN of excess fat and sinew. If using bamboo skewers, soak for several hours in water before using; this prevents them from burning. Prepare grill.

1 In a large mixing bowl, combine the turmeric, paprika, garam masala, cardamom, coriander, onion, garlic, lemon juice, sugar, salt and yogurt.

Stir mixture until well combined, adding a few drops of red food coloring, if desired.

2 Cut the chicken into long strips, about ¾-inch wide. Add chicken strips to the marinade; stir until the chicken is well coated. Cover and refrigerate for 3 hours or overnight, stirring occasionally. Remove chicken from marinade; reserve marinade.

4 Thread chicken onto skewers. Place skewers on lightly greased grill. Cook over medium-hot coals for about 8–10 minutes or until tender and well browned. Turn often and brush with reserved marinade several times during cooking.

1

2

3

CHILI CHICKEN WITH SALSA

Preparation time: 10 minutes +
   3 hours marinating
Total cooking time: 30 minutes
Serves 4

8 chicken thighs
   (about 1¼–1½ lb)
½ cup lemon juice
¼ teaspoon bottled crushed
   red chili peppers
2 tablespoons vegetable oil
2 teaspoons sesame oil
3 tablespoons soy sauce
3 tablespoons honey
1 clove garlic, crushed

2 green onions, chopped
3 tablespoons finely chopped
   fresh cilantro
salt, to taste

Salsa
1 small cucumber, chopped
1 small red onion, finely
   chopped
1 medium tomato, chopped
2 tablespoons olive oil
1 tablespoon white wine vinegar
¼ teaspoon sugar
¼ cup chopped fresh cilantro

TRIM CHICKEN of excess fat; remove skin, if desired.

1 In a bowl, combine lemon juice, chili pepper, oils, soy sauce, honey,

garlic, green onion, cilantro and salt; mix well. Add chicken, stir to combine. Cover with plastic wrap; refrigerate 3 hours or overnight; stir occasionally.

2 Prepare and oil the grill. Drain chicken; reserve marinade. Place chicken on the grill. Cook over medium heat for 10–15 minutes each side or until tender and cooked through. Brush with reserved marinade in the last 5 minutes of cooking. Serve hot with Salsa.

3 **To make Salsa:** Combine all salsa ingredients in a medium bowl and mix well.

COOK'S FILE

Storage time: Salsa can be made a day ahead. Serve at room temperature.

1

2

3

*Tandoori Chicken on skewers (top)
and Chili Chicken with Salsa*

GARLIC CHICKEN KEBABS WITH TOMATO AND MUSHROOM SALAD

Preparation time: 20 minutes
Total cooking time: 15 minutes
Makes 12

6 boneless, skinned chicken
   thighs (about 1 1/2 lb)
1 medium red pepper, cut into
   1-inch pieces
1 medium green pepper, cut into
   1-inch pieces
1 medium red onion, cut into
   small wedges
1/2 cup olive oil
2 cloves garlic, crushed
1 tablespoon chopped fresh
   chives
1 tablespoon chopped fresh
   mint
1 tablespoon chopped fresh
   thyme
1/2 teaspoon seasoned pepper
12 (10–12-inch) skewers

Tomato and Mushroom Salad
8 oz cherry tomatoes
4 oz mushrooms, quartered
1/4 cup olive oil
2 tablespoons white wine
   vinegar
1 clove garlic, crushed
salt, to taste
1 tablespoon chopped fresh
   chives
1 tablespoon chopped fresh mint
1 tablespoon chopped fresh
   thyme

PREPARE GRILL or preheat broiler.
Oil grill or broiler rack pan. If using
bamboo skewers, soak in water for
several hours before using.

1 Trim chicken of excess fat; cut into
1-inch pieces.
2 Thread chicken, red and green
peppers and onion alternately onto
skewers. In a small bowl, combine oil,
garlic, herbs and pepper.
3 To grill, place kebabs on lightly
oiled grill. Grill about 5-inches from
medium-hot coals until cooked through,
about 10–15 minutes. Turn and baste
with herb mixture 2 or 3 times.
To broil, place skewers on broiler pan,
about 4 inches from heat, and broil for
10–15 minutes or until cooked
through. Turn and baste with herb
mixture 2 or 3 times. Serve hot with
Tomato and Mushroom Salad.
**To make Tomato and Mushroom
Salad:** In a medium bowl combine
tomatoes and mushrooms. In a screw-
top jar combine oil, vinegar, garlic,
salt and herbs. Shake to mix well.
Pour over salad; toss to mix well.

CURRY, COCONUT AND LIME DRUMSTICKS

Preparation time: 10 minutes +
   3 hours marinating
Total cooking time: 20 minutes
Serves 4

melted butter or margarine
8 chicken drumsticks
   (about 2–2¹/₂ lb)
2 tablespoons curry paste or
   2–3 teaspoons curry powder
   (see note on page 65)

1 tablespoon grated lime rind
3 tablespoons lime juice
²/₃ cup canned coconut milk
1 tablespoon honey
salt, to taste
¹/₄ cup grated coconut

LINE A BAKING sheet with foil;
brush with melted butter or oil.
Prepare broiler; oil broiler rack.
1 Pull skin up and over joint of the
drumstick; secure with toothpicks.
2 Make three deep cuts into the
thickest section of the drumstick.
Combine curry paste or powder,

1 teaspoon of the lime rind, lime juice,
coconut milk and honey in a large
bowl. Add salt, if desired. Add
chicken; coat well. Store, covered, in
refrigerator 3 hours or overnight; stir
occasionally. Drain; reserve marinade.
3 Place drumsticks on prepared
broiler pan. Broil 8–10 minutes each
side or until cooked through, brushing
occasionally with reserved marinade.
Discard toothpicks.
4 Combine the coconut and remaining
lime rind; sprinkle over the chicken.
Serve chicken drumsticks hot.

GRILLED CHICKEN WINGS

Preparation time: 10 minutes +
  2 hours marinating
Total cooking time: 12 minutes
Serves 4 to 6

12 chicken wings
  (about 2½–3 lb)
3 tablespoons soy sauce
3 tablespoons hoisin sauce
½ cup tomato sauce
2 tablespoons honey
1 tablespoon brown sugar
1 tablespoon cider vinegar

2 cloves garlic, crushed
¼ teaspoon Chinese five-spice
  powder
salt, to taste
2 teaspoons sesame oil

RINSE CHICKEN wings and pat dry with paper towels.

1 Tuck wing tips to underside. Combine all the remaining ingredients in a large bowl; mix well.

2 Add wings and mix well to coat. Store, covered with plastic wrap, in refrigerator 2 hours or overnight; turn occasionally. Drain; reserve marinade.

3 Preheat broiler; oil broiler rack. Place wings on a cold, lightly-oiled broiler rack. Broil 4 inches from heat about 6 minutes on each side or until tender and cooked through, brushing with reserved marinade several times during cooking. Serve hot or cold as an appetizer.

COOK'S FILE

Storage time: Chicken Wings can be made up to 1 day in advance. Store, covered, in the refrigerator. Reheat in a moderate oven or in a microwave on medium/high for 2–3 minutes.

Note: Hoisin sauce, sesame oil and Chinese five-spice powder are available at most supermarkets. For note on five-spice powder, see page 81.

GINGER-CHILI DRUMSTICKS WITH CUCUMBER YOGURT

Preparation time: 10 minutes +
  3 hours marinating
Total cooking time: 20 minutes
Serves 6

1 tablespoon grated fresh ginger
1 tablespoon brown sugar
1 teaspoon bottled crushed
  red chili peppers
¼ teaspoon ground
  turmeric
1 teaspoon lemon juice
1 teaspoon finely grated lemon
  rind

1 cup plain yogurt
12 drumsticks (about 3 lb)

Cucumber Yogurt
1 cup plain yogurt
½ teaspoon bottled crushed red
  chili peppers
1 medium cucumber, finely
  chopped
½ teaspoon sugar
Salt, to taste

PREPARE BROILER. Oil the rack of broiler pan.

1 In a large bowl combine the ginger, brown sugar, crushed chili pepper, turmeric, lemon juice and lemon rind. Stir in yogurt; mix well. Add the chicken drumsticks, stirring well to coat with marinade. Cover with plastic wrap and refrigerate for 3 hours or overnight, stirring occasionally. Drain chicken; reserve marinade.

2 Place drumsticks on prepared broiler pan. Broil 5 inches from heat for 8–10 minutes on each side, brushing frequently with marinade, until cooked through. Serve hot or cold with Cucumber Yogurt.

3 To make Cucumber Yogurt: Combine yogurt, crushed chili pepper, cucumber, sugar and salt; mix well.

COOK'S FILE

Variation: For a cooler-flavored sauce, omit the chili from the cucumber yogurt and replace with 1 teaspoon of chopped fresh mint.

Grilled Chicken Wings (top)
and Ginger-Chili Drumsticks with Cucumber Yogurt

CHICKEN SATAY WITH PEANUT SAUCE

Preparation time: 30 minutes +
  2 hours marinating
Total cooking time: 35 minutes
Makes 12

2 lb boneless, skinned chicken
  thighs
1/3 cup soy sauce
2 tablespoons honey
3 tablespoons oil
24 (10–12 inch) skewers

Peanut Sauce
1 tablespoon oil
1 tablespoon minced onion
1 cup crunchy peanut butter
2/3 cup canned coconut milk
2/3 cup water

1 tablespoon soy sauce
1/4 cup chili sauce

TRIM EXCESS fat from chicken. If using bamboo skewers, soak in water for several hours before using.

1 Cut chicken into 3/4-inch strips. Place in a shallow glass or ceramic dish. Combine soy sauce, honey and oil and pour over chicken. Refrigerate, covered with plastic wrap, for 2 hours, turning occasionally.

2 To make Peanut Sauce: In a small saucepan, heat the oil over medium heat; add the onion. Sauté until tender. Remove from heat. Add peanut butter and coconut milk; blend well. Add water, soy sauce and chili sauce; mix well. Cook over low heat until heated through. Makes about 2 1/3 cups sauce.

3 Prepare and oil grill. Drain chicken and reserve marinade. Thread chicken onto skewers. Place the satay sticks on oiled grid of grill. Cook over medium-hot coals for about 10–12 minutes, turning often and brushing occasionally with reserved marinade. Serve immediately with Peanut Sauce and crunchy fried noodles, if desired.

COOK'S FILE:

Storage time: Chicken Satay can be refrigerated in the marinade for up to 8 hours. Assemble and grill just before serving. Peanut sauce can be made up to 8 hours ahead. Store in refrigerator. If too thick, thin with a little water when reheating. For appetizer servings, use 48 (6-inch) skewers and use less meat on each skewer. Proceed as above; serve with Peanut Sauce as a dip.

1

2

3

CORIANDER CHICKEN WITH TABOULI

Preparation time: 30 minutes
  + 1 hour marinating
Total cooking time: 14 minutes
Serves 4

4 boneless, skinned chicken
   breast halves (about 1 lb)
1/3 cup lime juice
2 tablespoons water
1 tablespoon sesame oil
2 tablespoons crushed coriander
   seeds

Tabouli
1/2 cup bulghur or cracked
   wheat
1/2 cup hot water

1 bunch flat leaf parsley
2 green onions, finely chopped
2 medium tomatoes, chopped
3 tablespoons lemon juice
3 tablespoons olive oil
salt, to taste

TRIM CHICKEN of any excess fat.
1 Place chicken breasts in a shallow, glass or ceramic dish. Combine the lime juice, water, sesame oil and coriander seeds; pour over the chicken. Place, covered with plastic wrap, in the refrigerator for 1 hour; turn occasionally.
2 To make Tabouli: In a medium bowl combine bulghur and hot water. Let stand 10 minutes, or until all the water is absorbed.
3 Finely chop the parsley. Add to bulghur with green onion, tomatoes,

lemon juice, olive oil and salt; mix well.
4 Prepare and oil grill. Drain chicken and reserve marinade. Place the chicken breasts on the oiled grill. Grill over medium-hot coals for 5–7 minutes on each side, brushing occasionally with reserved marinade, until cooked through and no longer pink. Serve with Tabouli.

COOK'S FILE

Storage time: Chicken can be refrigerated in the marinade for up to 8 hours. Cook just before serving.

BROILED GARLIC AND ROSEMARY CHICKEN

Preparation time: 10 minutes
+ 3 hours marinating
Total cooking time: 40 minutes
Serves 4

4 chicken legs (drumstick and
   thigh, about 2–2¹/₂ lb)
1 orange
¹/₂ cup orange juice
²/₃ cup olive oil
3 cloves garlic, finely
   chopped
2 tablespoons chopped fresh
   rosemary

1 tablespoon chopped fresh
   thyme
2 teaspoons Dijon mustard
salt to taste

TRIM CHICKEN of excess fat and
sinew. Remove skin if desired. Rinse
and pat dry with paper towels.

1 Using a sharp knife, make
3 or 4 deep cuts into the thickest part
of the chicken pieces.

2 Using a vegetable peeler, remove
long strips of rind from half the orange.

3 Combine the orange rind, orange
juice, oil, garlic, rosemary, thyme,
mustard and salt in a small bowl.
Place the chicken in a large shallow
baking dish. Pour the garlic-herb

mixture over the chicken. Cover with
plastic wrap and refrigerate 3 hours or
overnight, turning occasionally.

4 Preheat broiler. Line broiler pan
rack with foil; brush with melted
butter. Drain chicken and reserve
marinade. Place chicken on the
prepared broiler pan. Broil 5 inches
from the heat for 15–20 minutes each
side or until tender and cooked
through, brushing with reserved
marinade several times during
cooking. Garnish with slices of orange
and sprigs of rosemary, if desired.

CHICKEN WITH ORANGE-CHIVE BUTTER

Preparation time: 20 minutes +
2 hours marinating
Total cooking time: 24 minutes
Serves 4

8 medium chicken thigh cutlets
(about 2–2¹/₂ lb)
¹/₂ cup orange juice
1 teaspoon ground black pepper
2 teaspoons sesame oil

Orange-Chive Butter
¹/₂ cup butter or margarine
1 teaspoon finely grated orange
rind
1 tablespoon finely chopped
chives

1 tablespoon orange marmalade
salt, to taste

TRIM CHICKEN OF excess fat. Rinse
and pat dry with paper towels.
1 Place chicken in a shallow glass or
ceramic dish. Combine orange juice,
pepper and sesame oil; pour over
chicken. Cover with plastic wrap and
refrigerate 2 hours; turn occasionally.
Preheat broiler. Line broiler pan rack
with foil; brush with melted butter or
oil. Drain chicken and reserve
marinade. Place chicken on prepared
broiler pan. Broil 5 inches from heat
for 10–12 minutes on each side,
brushing occasionally with the
reserved marinade until cooked
through and no longer pink near bone.
Serve chicken immediately with slices
of Orange-Chive Butter.

2 To make Orange-Chive
Butter: Allow butter to soften
slightly at room temperature. Place in
a small mixing bowl; beat with a
wooden spoon for 1 minute, until
creamy. Add remaining ingredients
and mix until well combined.
3 Place butter mixture on a sheet of
plastic wrap and form into a log
shape. Roll up tightly and refrigerate
until required. Slice to serve.

COOK'S FILE

Storage time: Chicken can be
refrigerated in the marinade for up to
8 hours. Cook just before serving.
Orange-Chive Butter can be stored for
up to 2 days in the refrigerator, or
2 weeks in the freezer. Allow frozen
butter to thaw completely before
slicing and serving.

1

2

3

SOUTHERN-STYLE DRUMSTICKS

Preparation time: 15 minutes +
 4 hours marinating
Total cooking time: 25 minutes
Serves 4

8 drumsticks (about 2-2^1/2 lb)
^{2}/3 cup buttermilk
2 cloves garlic, crushed
1 teaspoon ground cumin
^{1}/4 teaspoon cayenne pepper
^{1}/4 teaspoon salt
^{1}/4 teaspoon black pepper

2 ears of corn, halved
2 tablespoons butter
4 drops tabasco sauce

TRIM CHICKEN of excess fat; rinse and pat dry with paper towels.

1 Place drumsticks in a shallow glass or ceramic dish. Combine buttermilk, garlic, cumin, cayenne pepper, salt and black pepper; pour over chicken. Cover with plastic wrap. Refrigerate for 4 hours; turn occasionally. Drain.

2 Prepare and oil the grill. Place the chicken drumsticks on grill. Grill over medium heat for 25–30 minutes, turning occasionally, until chicken is cooked through and no longer pink near bone. Serve immediately with cooked corn.

3 Cook corn in a large pan of boiling water, covered, for 2–3 minutes. Drain and place corn on individual pieces of foil. Melt butter; add red pepper sauce. Brush liberally on corn. Wrap corn in the foil; place on grill for 10 minutes, turning occasionally.

COOK'S FILE

Storage time: Chicken can be refrigerated in marinade overnight. Cook just before serving. Corn is best cooked just before serving.

1

2

3

GRILLED CHICKEN WITH FETA

Preparation time: 15 minutes +
  4 hours marinating
Total cooking time: 16 minutes
Serves 6

6 boneless, skinned chicken
  breast halves
  (about 1¼–1½ lb)
1 cup plain yogurt
3 tablespoons olive oil
3 tablespoons lemon juice
½ teaspoon ground oregano
salt, to taste
¼ teaspoon black pepper
3 oz feta cheese

TRIM CHICKEN of excess fat. Place in a shallow glass or ceramic dish.
1 Combine yogurt, olive oil, lemon juice, oregano, salt and pepper; pour over chicken. Refrigerate, covered with plastic wrap, for 4 hours, turning occasionally. Drain; reserve marinade.
2 Prepare broiler; brush broiler rack lightly with melted butter or oil. Broil chicken 4 inches from heat for 5–7 minutes each side, or until tender, cooked through and no longer pink.

Brush chicken with reserved marinade occasionally while cooking.
3 Slice feta thinly, and lay pieces across chicken breast pieces. Broil for 2 minutes or until cheese starts to bubble slightly. Serve immediately, with grilled baby eggplant or a salad of tomato, olives, green pepper, onion rings and lettuce.

COOK'S FILE

Storage time: Chicken can be refrigerated in marinade for up to 8 hours. Cook just before serving.
Variation: Use goat cheese instead of feta cheese in this recipe.

CHICKEN TERIYAKI

Preparation time: 20 minutes +
2 hours marinating
Total cooking time: 8 minutes
Makes 12

1½ lb chicken tenderloins
⅓ cup soy sauce
3 tablespoons mirin
(optional)
3 tablespoons sherry
3 tablespoons brown sugar
2 teaspoons grated fresh ginger
12 (10–12 inch) skewers
1 medium sweet red pepper, cut
into ¾-inch squares
4 green onions, cut into 1-inch
lengths
3 tablespoons vegetable oil

TRIM CHICKEN of excess fat.

1 Place chicken in a shallow glass or ceramic dish. Combine soy sauce, mirin, sherry, brown sugar and ginger. Stir to dissolve sugar; pour over chicken. Cover and refrigerate for up to 2 hours, turning occasionally. If using bamboo skewers, soak in water several hours before using. Prepare and oil the grill. Drain and cut tenderloins in half lengthwise.

2 Thread chicken onto skewers alternating with red pepper and green onion pieces. Brush kebabs with oil and place on grill.

3 Grill over medium-high heat for 6–8 minutes or until tender, turning and brushing with oil occasionally. Serve immediately, with steamed rice or Japanese-style egg noodles and stir-fried or grilled vegetables.

COOK'S FILE

Storage time: Chicken Teriyaki can be assembled and refrigerated in marinade for up to 4 hours. Cook just before serving.

1

2

3

BARBECUED HONEY CHICKEN WINGS

Preparation time: 10 minutes +
2 hours marinating
Total cooking time: 14 minutes
Serves 4

12 chicken wings
(about 2¹/2–3 lb)
¹/3 cup soy sauce
1 clove garlic, crushed
3 tablespoons sherry
3 tablespoons vegetable oil
3 tablespoons honey

RINSE CHICKEN wings and pat dry with paper towels. Tuck the wing tips to underside.

1 Place chicken wings in a shallow glass or ceramic dish. Combine the soy sauce, garlic, sherry and oil; pour over chicken.

2 Cover dish with plastic wrap and refrigerate for 2 hours, turning occasionally. Prepare and oil the grill. Drain the chicken and place on the oiled grill. Place the honey in a small heatproof cup or bowl on the edge of the grill to warm and thin down a little. Grill the chicken wings for 12 minutes or until tender and cooked through, turning occasionally.

3 Brush wings with honey and grill for 2 minutes more. Serve immediately.

COOK'S FILE

Variation: Substitute apricot jam for the honey, if desired. If you prefer a slightly hotter marinade, add some bottled crushed chili pepper to taste

SNACKS SOUPS & SALADS

CHICKEN AND LEEK PASTRIES

Preparation time: 40 minutes
Total cooking time: 38 minutes
Makes 20

1 tablespoon vegetable oil
3 boneless, skinned chicken
   thighs (about 9 oz)
1 slice bacon, chopped
2 medium leeks, thinly sliced
1 clove garlic, crushed
1/3 cup dry white wine
1/3 cup heavy cream
2 teaspoons prepared mustard
1/3 cup grated Parmesan cheese
salt and pepper
10 sheets phyllo, thawed
   according to package
   directions
1/3 cup butter or margarine, melted

PREHEAT OVEN to 400°F.
1 In a large skillet heat oil. Cook chicken over medium heat for 5–10 minutes on each side, or until browned and tender. Remove from pan and drain on paper towels. Cool; finely chop chicken.

2 Add bacon, leek and garlic to skillet; cook 3–4 minutes or until leek is soft and bacon crisp. Add chopped chicken, wine, cream and mustard. Cook, stirring constantly, 4 minutes or until slightly thickened. Remove from heat; stir in Parmesan cheese. Season with salt and pepper to taste; cool slightly.
3 Lay one sheet of phyllo on a flat work surface. Brush sheet with melted butter. Top with another sheet; brush with butter. Cut the pastry evenly lengthwise into four strips. Place 1 tablespoon of chicken mixture at one end of each strip. Fold one corner of strip diagonally over filling so short end meets long end of strip, forming a right angle. Continue folding at right angles, until strip ends. Repeat with remaining lengths of phyllo and filling. Place seam-side down, on baking sheet. Brush with melted butter. Bake 20 minutes, or until pastry is golden and filling is hot.

COOK'S FILE

Storage time: Uncooked pastries can be kept overnight in the refrigerator. To freeze, seal in an airtight container for up to 2 months. Cook pastries just before serving.

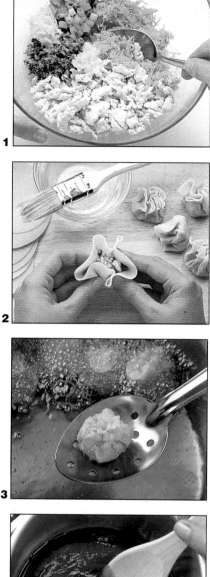

CHICKEN WONTONS WITH PLUM SAUCE

Preparation time: 20 minutes
Total cooking time: 15 minutes
Makes about 30

1 tablespoon vegetable oil
6 oz ground raw chicken
1/3 cup finely shredded
   carrot
2 green onions, finely
   chopped
1 tablespoon finely chopped
   fresh cilantro
1 tablespoon soy sauce
1 teaspoon grated fresh ginger
1 clove garlic, crushed
1 teaspoon sesame oil
1/2 teaspoon sugar
Salt, to taste
8 oz (about 30) round or square
   wonton wrappers
Oil for deep-frying

Plum sauce
1 cup bottled plum sauce
1 tablespoon soy sauce

HEAT OIL in skillet or saucepan. Cook chicken over medium heat until no longer pink.

1 Combine cooked chicken, carrot, green onions, cilantro, soy sauce, ginger, garlic, sesame oil, sugar and salt; mix well.

2 Place 1 rounded teaspoon of mixture into center of each wonton wrapper. Brush edges of wrapper with a little water, bring together to form little bundles and squeeze gently to secure. In a large heavy saucepan, add oil to 1 3/4–2-inch depth.

3 Heat the oil. Lower the chicken bundles into the hot oil, 2 or 3 at a time. Cook until golden, crisp, and cooked through, 1–2 minutes. Remove from oil with a slotted spoon, drain on paper towels; keep warm. Serve the wontons hot with Plum Sauce.

4 To make Plum Sauce: In a small saucepan combine plum sauce and soy sauce. Cook and stir over medium heat until heated through.

COOK'S FILE

Storage time: Wontons can be assembled up to Step 3 a day ahead. Refrigerate, covered well in plastic wrap or stored in an airtight container, to prevent drying out. Cook just before serving.

Note: Wonton wrappers are available from Asian food stores.

SPICY CHICKEN MINI TURNOVERS

Preparation time: 30 minutes
Total cooking time: 30 minutes
Makes 20

2 tablespoons vegetable oil
1 small onion, finely chopped
1 clove garlic, crushed
1/2 teaspoon ground coriander
1/2 teaspoon ground cumin
1/4 teaspoon ground turmeric
1/4 teaspoon chili powder
1/2 lb ground raw chicken

1/2 cup frozen peas
1 tablespoon chopped fresh
   cilantro
salt and pepper
5 sheets frozen puff pastry
1 large egg, beaten

PREHEAT OVEN to 375°F. Line two baking sheets with foil; set aside.
1 In a large pan, heat oil. Add onion and garlic. Stir in coriander; cumin, turmeric and chili powder; stir until onions are soft. Add chicken; sauté over medium-high heat until browned. Continue cooking over low heat until liquid evaporates; stir occasionally.

2 Stir in peas, cilantro and salt and pepper to taste. Remove from heat; cool.
3 On a lightly floured surface, cut 20, 4¹/2 inch rounds from the puff pastry. Place one tablespoon chicken filling in the center of each circle. Fold in half and seal edge. Place 10 turnovers on each prepared baking sheet; brush with beaten egg. Bake 15–20 minutes or until golden.

COOK'S FILE

Storage time: Turnovers can be prepared several hours ahead. Store, covered, in the refrigerator and then bake just before serving.

1

2

3

ORIENTAL CHICKEN NOODLE SOUP

Preparation time: 30 minutes
Total cooking time: 15 minutes
Serves 6

½ cup dried Chinese
   mushrooms
5 oz fresh Chinese egg
   noodles
½ bunch bok choy
1 tablespoon peanut oil
2 tablespoons sesame oil
1 medium onion, chopped
6 cups chicken broth or stock
3 tablespoons soy sauce
1 tablespoon fresh grated
   ginger
1 clove garlic, crushed
4 (about 1 lb) boneless, skinned
   chicken breast halves,
   thinly sliced
8 oz fresh or frozen baby corn
1 large red sweet pepper, cut in
   thin strips

SOAK MUSHROOMS in boiling water for 20 minutes. Drain and squeeze out excess liquid. Thinly slice; set aside. Cook noodles in rapidly boiling water until just tender. Rinse; drain well.

1 Cut leaves from stems of bok choy. Cut stems into 1-inch lengths; chop leaves. In large saucepan, heat peanut oil and sesame oil. Add onion and bok choy stems; cook over medium heat, stirring, for 3 minutes or until onion and stems are just tender.

2 Add the chicken broth, soy sauce, ginger and garlic to pan. Bring to a boil, stirring occasionally. Add chicken. Reduce the heat and simmer, for 4 minutes, or until chicken is just cooked through.

3 Cut the baby corn into ¾ inch lengths. Add to the broth mixture along with the strips of red pepper,

bok choy leaves and mushrooms. Bring to a boil; reduce the heat and simmer for 3 minutes or until the red pepper and bok choy leaves are tender—do not overcook. To serve, place the drained, hot noodles in the bottom of each serving bowl. Pour the soup over the noodles.

COOK'S FILE

Storage time: Soup and noodles can be prepared one day ahead. Store separately in airtight containers in the refrigerator. To reheat noodles, immerse in boiling water for about 30 seconds; drain well. Reheat soup just until hot; do not overcook.

1

2

3

CHICKEN AND COCONUT MILK SOUP

Preparation time: 30 minutes
Total cooking time: 12 minutes
Serves 8

5 oz rice sticks or rice
  vermicelli
rind of 1 lime
2–4 red or green chili peppers,
  seeded and chopped
1 medium onion, chopped
2 cloves garlic, crushed
1 tablespoon grated fresh
  ginger
2 stalks lemongrass,
  chopped
1 tablespoon chopped fresh
  cilantro
1 tablespoon peanut oil
4 green onions, chopped
4 cups chicken broth or
  stock
1 can (14 oz) coconut milk
1 lb boneless, skinned chicken
  breast, cut into thin strips
4 oz tofu, cubed
1¼ cups fresh bean sprouts
1 tablespoon brown sugar

POUR BOILING water over the rice
sticks or vermicelli to cover. Let stand
5 minutes; drain. Cut into shorter
lengths and set aside.

1 Cut the lime rind into long, very
thin strips with a sharp knife.

2 In a blender container or food
processor bowl, combine the chili
pepper, onion, garlic, ginger,
lemongrass and cilantro. Blend or
process the mixture until smooth.

3 In a large saucepan, heat the
peanut oil over medium heat. Add the
processed chili pepper mixture and
the green onions; cook for 3 minutes,
stirring frequently. Add chicken
broth, coconut milk and lime strips;
bring mixture to a boil. Add the
chicken and cook for 4 minutes or
until chicken is tender.

4 Stir in tofu, bean sprouts and
brown sugar. Stir over medium heat
until heated through. To serve, place
the noodles into soup bowls; pour
soup over noodles. Garnish with
thinly sliced red chili pepper and
whole cilantro leaves, if desired.

COOK'S FILE

Storage time: Chicken and Coconut
Milk Soup can be made 1 day in
advance, up to Step 4. Just before
serving, cook noodles, reheat soup and
add remaining ingredients.

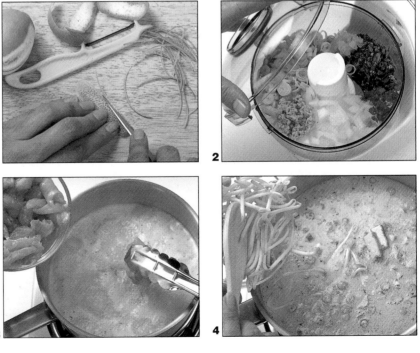

WARM CHICKEN SALAD

Preparation time: 20 minutes
Total cooking time: 25 minutes
Serves 4 to 6

2 large sweet red peppers
6 boneless, skinned chicken
   thighs (about 1–1$\frac{1}{4}$ lb)
1 tablespoon oil
$\frac{3}{4}$ lb fresh green beans
leaf lettuce or red leaf lettuce,
   torn (about 6 cups)
1 cup crumbed feta cheese

Garlic Mustard Vinaigrette
$\frac{1}{2}$ cup olive oil
1 tablespoon balsamic
   vinegar
3 tablespoons white wine
   vinegar
1 clove garlic, crushed
1 tablespoon Dijon mustard
salt and pepper

CUT RED PEPPERS into quarters. Discard seeds and membranes. Place skin-side up on foil-lined baking sheet. Brush with oil.

1 Broil peppers about 5 inches from heat for 12–15 minutes or until skin is black. Cover with paper towels until cool. Peel off skins and cut peppers into $\frac{1}{4}$-inch strips.

2 Trim chicken of excess fat. Cut into long thin strips. Trim beans and cut into 2-inch lengths. In large skillet, heat oil. Cook chicken, in 2 batches, over medium-high heat for 3 minutes or until browned and cooked through. Remove from pan; drain on paper towels.

3 Add beans to pan and cook until just tender. Add chicken and red pepper to pan just to reheat. Serve warm on a bed of lettuce leaves, topped with crumbled feta cheese. Just before serving, drizzle with Garlic Mustard Vinaigrette.

4 To make Garlic Mustard Vinaigrette: Place all ingredients in a small screw-top jar; shake well.

COOK'S FILE

Storage time: Salad is best made just before serving, but vinaigrette can be made several days ahead. Store in refrigerator. Shake well before use. If desired, roast red peppers ahead also. Store in an airtight container in refrigerator up to 3 days.

CREAM OF CHICKEN AND VEGETABLE SOUP

Preparation time: 20 minutes
Total cooking time: 1 hour 45 minutes
Serves 6

1 x 2–2¹/₂ lb broiler-fryer
   chicken

Stock
6 cups water
¹/₂ stalk celery, chopped
6 peppercorns
1 bay leaf
1 clove garlic, chopped
1 small onion, chopped

Soup
1 medium carrot

¹/₃ cup unsifted all-purpose flour
³/₄ cup milk
1 tablespoon vegetable oil
1 medium onion, sliced
2 cups sliced fresh mushrooms
1¹/₄ cups light cream
¹/₂ package (6 oz) frozen pea
   pods, thinly sliced lengthwise
3 medium tomatoes, peeled,
   seeded, chopped
1 tablespoon soy sauce
salt and pepper

REMOVE EXCESS fat from chicken. Rinse and pat dry with paper towels.
1 Cut chicken into breast, thigh, leg and wing pieces.
2 To make Stock: In a large saucepan or Dutch oven, combine water, celery, peppercorns, bay leaf, garlic and onion. Add chicken pieces.

Bring to boil; reduce heat and simmer, covered, for 1¹/₄ hours. Remove from heat; cool slightly. Strain, reserve stock and chicken; discard onion mixture. (You need 5 cups chicken stock for this recipe). Remove chicken from bones; discard bones and skin. Cut chicken into thin strips; set aside.
3 To make Soup: Cut carrot into matchstick-size pieces. In a small bowl combine flour and milk; mix well. Heat oil in Dutch oven; add onion, carrot and mushrooms. Cook, stirring over low heat until onion is tender; stir in 5 cups broth and milk mixture. Bring to a boil. Reduce the heat and simmer, stirring, until slightly thickened. Stir in chicken strips, cream, pea pods, tomatoes and soy sauce; heat through. Season to taste. Serve hot.

1

2

3

4

ITALIAN-STYLE CHICKEN PASTA SALAD

Preparation time: 30 minutes
 + 3 hours marinating
Total cooking time: 30 minutes
Serves 6 to 8

3 boneless, skinned chicken
 breast halves (about 12 oz)
1/4 cup lemon juice
1 clove garlic, crushed
3 oz thinly sliced prosciutto
1 medium cucumber
2 tablespoons seasoned pepper
2 tablespoons olive oil
1 1/2 cups penne pasta
1/2 cup sun-dried tomatoes, cut
 in thin strips
1/2 cup pitted black olives,
 halved
1/2 cup canned artichoke hearts,
 halved or quartered
2 oz Parmesan cheese, shaved
 into thin slices

Creamy Basil Dressing
1/2 cup olive oil
2 tablespoons white wine
 vinegar
1/4 teaspoon seasoned pepper
1 teaspoon Dijon mustard
1 tablespoon cornstarch
1/2 cup water

3/4 cup light cream
1/3 cup chopped fresh basil
salt, to taste

REMOVE EXCESS fat from chicken.
1 Place in a medium bowl with lemon juice and garlic. Cover with plastic wrap, and refrigerate for at least 3 hours or overnight, turning occasionally. Cut cucumber in half lengthwise and slice.
2 Drain chicken and sprinkle both sides with seasoned pepper. In large skillet, heat oil. Cook the chicken for 5 minutes on each side, or until lightly browned and cooked through. Remove from heat. Cool chicken and cut into 3/4-inch pieces.
3 Cook the pasta according to the package directions and drain well. Rinse the pasta and drain again. In a large bowl combine the pasta, chicken pieces, cucumber slices, prosciutto, sun-dried tomatoes, olives and artichoke hearts. Pour warm Creamy Basil Dressing over and toss gently to combine. Serve the salad warm or cold, sprinkled with Parmesan cheese shavings.
4 To make Creamy Basil Dressing: In a medium saucepan combine oil, vinegar, seasoned pepper and mustard. Combine cornstarch and water until smooth. Add to pan. Whisk over medium heat for 2 minutes,

or until the sauce boils and thickens. Add the cream, basil and salt. Stir until heated through.

COOK'S FILE

Storage time: Make dressing just before assembling salad. Chicken and pasta can be cooked a day ahead and stored, covered, in refrigerator.
Hint: Serve this salad with a large round Italian loaf or vegetable bread plus a bottle of chilled white wine.
Variation: Any small size pasta can be used instead of penne in this dish.

THAI CHICKEN SALAD

Preparation time: 20 minutes
Total cooking time: 10 minutes
Serves 6

1 head romaine lettuce
4 sprigs fresh cilantro
4 sprigs fresh mint
1 small red onion
3 green onions
2 tablespoons vegetable oil
1½ lb ground raw chicken
½ cup water
½ cup lime juice
3 tablespoons soy sauce
3 tablespoons fish sauce
1 tablespoon chili sauce

2 cloves garlic, crushed
2 teaspoons brown sugar
salt, to taste
1 tablespoon chopped fresh
   lemongrass
⅓ cup roasted peanuts
1 tablespoon fresh cilantro
   leaves, for garnish
1 tablespoon chopped roasted
   peanuts, for garnish

WASH AND DRY romaine leaves thoroughly. Arrange on serving platter.

1 Finely chop cilantro and mint. Cut red onion into thin slices and separate into rings. Chop green onions.

2 In large skillet, heat oil. Add ground chicken and water. Cook over medium heat 5–10 minutes or until cooked through and almost all liquid has evaporated. Break up any lumps. Remove from heat.

3 Transfer chicken to a medium bowl. Stir in cilantro, mint, red onion and green onions. Combine lime juice, soy, fish sauce, chili sauce, garlic, brown sugar, salt and lemongrass in a small bowl; mix well. Pour over chicken mixture. Chill. Just before serving, stir in peanuts. Serve on prepared lettuce leaves, sprinkled with additional cilantro leaves and peanuts.

COOK'S FILE

Storage time: Recipe can be made up to Step 3 a day ahead. Store in an airtight container in the refrigerator. Assemble just before serving.

1

2

3

CURRIED CHICKEN, APPLE, AND CELERY SALAD

Preparation time: 30 minutes
Total cooking time: 40 minutes
Serves 8

4 chicken legs (drumstick and thigh, about 2–2¹/₂ lb)
1¹/₄ cups orange juice
2¹/₂ cups water
2 medium red apples
2 celery stalks
1¹/₄ cups green seedless grapes
³/₄ cup walnuts, chopped

Curry Mayonnaise
¹/₄ cup butter or margarine
1 small onion, finely chopped
1 tablespoon curry powder
¹/₂ cup mayonnaise
²/₃ cup sour cream
¹/₂ cup heavy cream
2 tablespoons lemon juice
1 tablespoon brown sugar
salt, to taste

TRIM CHICKEN of excess fat and sinew.

1 Place chicken in a large saucepan. Add orange juice and water. Cover; bring to boil. Reduce heat and simmer, covered, until chicken is tender, about 30–35 minutes. Remove from heat. Drain and cool. Remove chicken meat from bones; cut into ³/₄-inch pieces. Discard skin and bones.

2 Cut apples in half, remove cores; cut into ¹/₂-inch cubes. Slice celery. In a large bowl, combine chicken, apple, celery, grapes and walnuts.

3 **To make Curry Mayonnaise:** In a small saucepan, melt butter. Cook onion until soft. Stir in curry powder, cook 30 seconds. Transfer to a small bowl. Add mayonnaise, sour cream, cream, lemon juice, brown sugar and salt; mix well. Gently fold into chicken mixture.

COOK'S FILE

Storage time: This salad can be prepared a day ahead. Cover tightly and refrigerate until ready to serve.

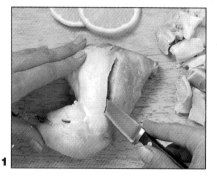

RASPBERRY CHICKEN SALAD

Preparation time: 15 minutes
Total cooking time: 10 minutes
Serves 4

4 boneless, skinned chicken breast halves
1 cup white wine
1 cup curly endive
1 red leaf lettuce
1 cup watercress
¹/₂ cup olive oil
2 tablespoons raspberry vinegar

¹/₂ teaspoon Dijon mustard
salt and freshly ground black pepper, to taste
1 pint raspberries

TRIM CHICKEN of any excess fat.

1 Pour wine into large heavy-based frying pan; add enough water to make liquid about 1-inch deep. Cover; bring to a boil. Reduce heat; add chicken to pan, cover and simmer for 10 minutes or until cooked through. Remove from pan. Drain, cool and cut into slices.

2 Wash and dry endive, lettuce and watercress. Tear into bite-size pieces, discarding thicker stems of watercress. Place into a large mixing bowl.

3 Place olive oil, vinegar, mustard and seasonings in a small screw-top jar and shake well. Pour one-third of dressing over leaves; toss lightly to combine. Place ¹/₃ cup of raspberries and the remaining dressing in food processor bowl. Using pulse action, process 10 seconds or until smooth. Arrange leaves on serving plates, top with chicken slices and remaining raspberries. Drizzle with raspberry dressing and serve immediately.

COOK'S FILE

Storage: Chicken may be poached 1 day in advance. Refrigerate, covered with plastic wrap, until required.

Curried Chicken, Apple and Celery Salad (top) and Raspberry Chicken Salad.

FAST CHICKEN

THAI CHICKEN

Preparation time: 20 minutes
Total cooking time: 15 minutes
Serves 4

1 lb boneless chicken thighs,
    skinned
2 tablespoons vegetable oil
2 large onions, cut into small
    wedges
1 tablespoon curry paste
    (see note below)
2 teaspoons grated fresh ginger
2 cloves garlic, crushed
1 stem lemongrass, finely
    chopped
1 tablespoon fish sauce
    (nam pla)
3 cups canned coconut milk
4 medium carrots, julienned
4 oz cut green beans
1/4 cup chopped fresh cilantro
1/4 cup chopped fresh mint
salt, to taste
hot cooked Chinese noodles or
    rice
1 cup toasted, flaked coconut

TRIM CHICKEN of excess fat and
sinew. Cut into thin strips.
1 In a large skillet or wok, heat
1 tablespoon of the oil. Add chicken
and stir-fry over medium-high heat for
2–3 minutes or until no pink remains.

Remove chicken from skillet. Drain on
paper towels. Heat remaining oil. Add
onion, curry paste, ginger and garlic.
Stir-fry over medium-high heat for
1 minute. Return chicken to skillet.
2 Add lemongrass, fish sauce,
coconut milk, carrots and green beans
to skillet; bring to a boil. Reduce heat;
simmer, uncovered, for 10 minutes or
until chicken and vegetables are
tender, stirring occasionally.
3 Stir in cilantro, mint and salt. Serve
immediately over noodles or rice.
Sprinkle with coconut.

COOK'S FILE

Storage time: This recipe can be
made a day ahead. Store, covered with
plastic wrap, in the refrigerator.
Note: Indian and Thai style curry
pastes are available at Asian food
stores and some large supermarkets.
These authentic blends contain a
mixture of fresh and dry herbs and
spices combined with vinegar, oil or
water. Curry powders are a blend of
dried, ground spices. Curry powders
and pastes vary in heat from mild to
hot. If paste is not available, substitute
2–3 teaspoons of curry powder.
Hint: Fresh lemongrass is also
available at Asian food stores—use
only the white stems. To release the
aromatic flavor, bruise the stem with
the back of a knife, or crush with a
rolling pin, then finely chop.

CAMEMBERT CHICKEN WITH CRANBERRY SAUCE

Preparation time: 10 minutes
Total cooking time: 15 minutes
Serves 4

4 large boneless chicken breast
    halves (about 1 lb)
1 package (4^1/$_2$ oz) camembert
    cheese, skinned
2 cloves garlic, crushed
2 tablespoons finely chopped
    fresh chives
all-purpose flour
2 tablespoons vegetable oil
1 cup white wine
^{1}/$_4$ cup wholeberry cranberry
    sauce
salt and pepper

TRIM CHICKEN of any excess fat
and sinew.

1 Using a small, sharp knife, cut a
deep pocket in each breast half, cutting
from edge into the thickest part of
chicken piece. Place the camembert
into a bowl and mash with a fork. Add
the garlic and chives; blend well.
Spoon the mixture into the chicken
breast pockets and secure the open-
ings with toothpicks. Toss the chicken
lightly in flour; shake off excess.

2 In a skillet, heat the oil. Add
chicken; brown over medium-high
heat for 1 minute on each side. Reduce
the heat and cook for 3–4 minutes on
each side or until the chicken is
cooked through. Remove from pan.
Cover chicken loosely with foil while
preparing sauce.

3 Add the wine and the cranberry
sauce to pan, stir well. Season to taste.
Cook over medium-high heat until
sauce has thickened and reduced by
half. Pour sauce over chicken and
serve immediately.

1

2

3

CHICKEN AND VEGETABLE CURRY

Preparation time: 5 minutes
Total cooking time: 15 minutes
Serves 4

2 medium boneless, skinned
    chicken breast halves
    (about 6 oz)
2 tablespoons oil
1/3 cup mild curry paste
    (see note on page 65)

1 package (16 oz) frozen mixed
    Oriental vegetables, thawed
2/3 cup water
1/2 cup plain yogurt
salt, to taste
hot cooked rice

RINSE CHICKEN and pat dry with paper towels.
1 Cut chicken into 3/4-inch cubes. In large skillet, heat oil.
2 Add chicken; cook over medium-high heat 4 minutes or until browned, stirring occasionally. Add curry paste

and vegetables to pan; mix well.
2 Add water to pan. Bring to a boil; reduce heat to a simmer and cook, covered, for 3–5 minutes or until vegetables and chicken are tender. Remove from heat, stir in yogurt. Add salt to taste and serve immediately with hot, cooked rice.

COOK'S FILE

Storage time: Cook this dish just before serving.
Variation: Use fresh, chopped vegetables instead of frozen in this recipe.

1

2

3

LEMON AND ROSEMARY CHICKEN

Preparation time: 10 minutes
Total cooking time: 30 minutes
Serves 4

8 chicken drumsticks
(about 2–2¹/₂ lb)
¹/₃ cup butter or margarine
2 cloves garlic, crushed
2 teaspoons finely grated lemon rind
2 tablespoons chopped fresh rosemary or 1–2 teaspoons dried rosemary

1 tablespoon unsifted all-purpose flour
1¹/₂ cups chicken broth or stock
2 tablespoons lemon juice
salt and pepper

RINSE CHICKEN and pat dry with paper towels.

1 Using a sharp knife, make two deep cuts in the thickest part of each chicken drumstick.

2 In a large skillet, melt the butter and add the drumsticks. Cook over medium-high heat for about 5 minutes on each side or until brown. Add the chopped garlic, grated lemon rind and fresh rosemary.

3 Combine flour, broth and lemon juice; mix until smooth. Add to pan; bring to a boil. Reduce heat and simmer, covered, for 25 minutes or until drumsticks are tender and no pink remains near bone, stirring occasionally. Season and serve immediately.

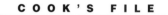

COOK'S FILE

Storage time: This recipe can be cooked up to a day ahead. Store, covered, in the refrigerator. Reheat gently just before serving.

Hint: To check whether chicken is cooked, insert a skewer into the thickest part of chicken. If juice runs clear the chicken is cooked.

1   2   3

CHILI CHICKEN WINGS

Preparation time: 10 minutes
Total cooking time: 16 minutes
Serves 4

1 medium sweet red pepper
1 medium green pepper
12 chicken wings
    (about 2–2½ lb)
1 large egg white, beaten
½ cup cornstarch
2 tablespoons soy sauce
3 tablespoons water
3 tablespoons vegetable oil
2 cloves garlic, crushed
2 teaspoons sambal oelek
    (Indonesian red chili sauce)
3 tablespoons black bean
    sauce
2 cups chicken broth or stock
½ cup roasted unsalted
    cashews, chopped

CUT PEPPERS into thin strips.
1 Cut the chicken wings into three sections, discarding tips.
2 Combine the egg white, cornstarch, soy sauce and water in a medium bowl; add the chicken wings and stir until combined.
3 Heat oil in a wok or large skillet. Add chicken wings and stir-fry over medium-high heat 8–10 minutes or until brown and cooked through. Remove chicken from pan and drain on paper towels.
4 Add the red and green pepper strips, garlic and sambal oelek to pan and stir-fry for 2 minutes or until peppers are tender. Add black bean sauce, broth and chicken. Bring to a boil; cover and cook 2 minutes or until chicken has heated through. Sprinkle cashews over and serve immediately. Serve Chili Chicken Wings with steamed rice, if desired.

COOK'S FILE

Storage time: Cook this dish just before serving.
Variation: Chopped, boneless chicken breast or thighs can be used instead of wings in this recipe. You can also serve this dish with fresh noodles instead of rice if preferred.
Hint: Sambal oelek is Indonesian crushed hot chilies in vinegar. It is available from most large supermarkets or Asian food stores.

1

2

3

4

CHICKEN WITH MUSHROOMS

Preparation time: 10 minutes
Total cooking time: 20 minutes
Serves 4

4 boneless, skinned chicken
    breast halves (about 1 lb)
2 tablespoons butter
2 tablespoons vegetable oil
4 small zucchini, thinly sliced
2 leeks, thinly sliced
2 cloves garlic, crushed
2 small red or green chili peppers,
    seeded and finely chopped

6 oz oyster mushrooms
1 tablespoon lime juice
1/3 cup light cream
salt and pepper

TRIM CHICKEN of excess fat and sinew.

1 In large skillet, heat butter and oil. Add chicken and cook over medium heat for 5 minutes on each side or until tender. Remove from pan; drain on paper towels and keep warm.

2 Add zucchini, leeks, garlic and chopped chilies to pan. Cook over medium-high heat for 2 minutes. Add mushrooms; cook 3 minutes or until the vegetables are tender.

3 Stir in the lime juice and cream. Return chicken to skillet; cook 2 minutes more until heated through. Season to taste. Serve immediately with roasted red peppers and warm crusty rolls, if desired.

COOK'S FILE

Storage time: Cook this dish just before serving.

Note: You can buy oyster mush-rooms at Asian stores. If not available, use button or cap mushrooms instead.

Hint: Wear rubber gloves when chopping chilies; rinse after chopping. Avoid touching your face, because chili oil can burn eyes and skin.

PAPRIKA CHICKEN DRUMSTICKS

Preparation time: 10 minutes
Total cooking time: 30 minutes
Serves 4

8 chicken drumsticks
    (about 2–2 1/2 lb)
1 tablespoon paprika
1 tablespoon vegetable oil
2 tablespoons butter or
    margarine
2 cups chicken broth or stock
3/4 cup tomato purée
2 large onions, cut in thin
    wedges
1/3 cup soft cream cheese

2 green onions, finely chopped
salt and pepper

RINSE DRUMSTICKS and pat dry with paper towels.

1 Sprinkle the chicken drumsticks evenly with paprika.

2 In large skillet, heat oil and butter; add chicken. Cook over medium-high heat for 5 minutes or until chicken is browned, turning occasionally. Remove from pan, drain on paper towels. Keep warm.

3 Add the chicken broth, tomato purée, onion wedges, cream cheese and green onions to the pan; bring to a boil. Reduce heat. Return the chicken to the pan and simmer, covered, for about 20–25 minutes or

until the chicken is tender; stir occasionally. Season to taste and serve immediately with hot fettuccini tossed with poppyseeds, if desired.

COOK'S FILE

Storage time: This dish can be cooked up to 2 days in advance. Store, covered, in refrigerator. Reheat just before serving.

Variations: Replace 1 cup of the broth with one cup of white wine.

Hint: After cooking any chicken dish ahead of time, cool it rapidly by immersing the base of the dish in iced water. Store, covered, in the refrigerator. Harmful bacteria can develop if the dish is left to cool slowly at room temperature.

Chicken with Mushrooms (top) and Paprika Chicken Drumsticks

ALMOND CHICKEN WITH BRANDY SAUCE

Preparation time: 10 minutes
Total cooking time: 20 minutes
Serves 4

4 boneless, skinned chicken
   breast halves (about 1 lb)
1 cup sliced almonds
3 tablespoons vegetable oil
1/4 cup butter or margarine
2 leeks, thinly sliced (white part
   only)
1/2 cup brandy or cognac

3/4 cup heavy cream
salt and pepper

TRIM CHICKEN of any excess fat and
sinew. Rinse chicken; pat dry with
paper towels.

1 In a large skillet, toast sliced
almonds over medium heat for about
3 minutes, stirring until golden.
Remove from pan, set aside.

2 Heat oil in pan; add chicken. Cook
over medium-high heat for 1 minute
on each side. Reduce heat; cook for
4–5 minutes more on each side or until
cooked through. Remove from pan;
keep warm. Drain any oil from pan.

3 Add the butter and sliced leeks to
the pan. Cook over medium heat for
3 minutes or until the leeks are tender.
Add the cognac or brandy to the pan
and cook until reduced by half,
stirring occasionally. Add cream, cook
for 3 minutes or until sauce has
thickened slightly. To serve, place
chicken on individual serving plates,
pour the sauce over chicken and
sprinkle with almonds. Serve hot with
a steamed vegetable.

COOK'S FILE

Storage time: Cook this dish just
before serving.

1

2

3

CHINESE CHICKEN AND NOODLES

Preparation time: 10 minutes
Total cooking time: 18 minutes
Serves 4

1 lb boneless, skinned chicken thighs
1/4 cup hoisin sauce
3 tablespoons dry sherry
1 tablespoon soy sauce
2 tablespoons vegetable oil
1 onion, cut into wedges
2 medium carrots, thinly sliced
1 1/2 cups snow pea pods
4 cups chopped bok choy or Chinese cabbage
1 tablespoon cornstarch

1 cup chicken broth or stock
2 cups fresh bean sprouts
3 oz fresh Chinese egg noodles

TRIM CHICKEN of any excess fat. Rinse and pat dry with paper towels.

1 Cut chicken into 3/4-inch cubes. In a large bowl combine hoisin sauce, sherry and soy sauce.

2 In a large skillet, heat the oil. Add the onion wedges and carrot; cook over medium-high heat for 3 minutes, stirring occasionally. Add the snow peas and bok choy or Chinese cabbage and cook, stirring, for 1 minute. Remove from pan; set aside.

3 Add chicken mixture to pan. Cook, stirring occasionally, over medium-high heat for 10 minutes or until chicken is tender and cooked through. Combine cornstarch and broth.

4 Return vegetables to pan. Add bean sprouts and cornstarch mixture to skillet. Stir 2 minutes or until sauce boils and thickens. Cook noodles in a medium pan of rapidly boiling water until just tender, about 2 minutes. Drain. Place noodles in individual deep serving plates or soup bowls. Spoon chicken and vegetables over noodles. Serve immediately.

COOK'S FILE

Storage time: Cook this dish just before serving.

STIR-FRIED CHICKEN AND VEGETABLES

Preparation time: 15 minutes
Total cooking time: 10 minutes
Serves 4

4 medium boneless, skinned chicken breast halves (about 12–14 oz)
2 tablespoons vegetable oil
1 medium green pepper, cut in thin strips
2 cloves garlic, crushed
2 teaspoons grated fresh ginger

8 cups sliced Chinese cabbage
1 package (6 oz) frozen pea pods or 1¹/₂ cups sugar snap peas
4 green onions, cut into 1-inch pieces
1¹/₄ cups light chicken broth
1 tablespoon cornstarch
1 tablespoon oyster sauce
1 tablespoon dry sherry
salt, to taste

TRIM CHICKEN of excess fat and sinew. Rinse and pat dry with paper towels. Slice chicken into thin strips
1 In large skillet or wok, heat oil. Add the chicken fillets and stir-fry over high heat 4 minutes or until browned.

Remove from pan; drain on paper towels. Keep warm.
2 Add pepper, garlic and ginger; stir-fry for 2 minutes. Add cabbage, pea pods and green onions; stir-fry for 1 minute. Return chicken to pan.
3 Combine broth, cornstarch, oyster sauce and sherry until smooth. Add to ingredients in pan. Stir over medium-high heat for 1–2 minutes or until sauce boils and thickens, and chicken and vegetables are tender. Add salt to taste, serve immediately.

COOK'S FILE

Storage time: Cook this dish just before serving.

CRISPY SPICED CHICKEN APPETIZER WINGS

Preparation time: 5 minutes
Total cooking time: 8 minutes
Serves 4 to 6

12 chicken wings
    (about 2–2¹/2 lb)
2 teaspoons ground cumin
2 teaspoons ground coriander
2 teaspoons ground cardamom
2 teaspoons ground turmeric
2 teaspoons chili powder
salt, to taste
oil for deep frying
¹/2 cup chutney

WIPE CHICKEN wings.
1 Pat dry with paper towels.
2 In a large bowl, combine cumin, coriander, cardamom, turmeric, chili powder and salt. Add chicken wings, toss to coat completely. Rub spice mixture into the chicken.
3 In a large saucepan or deep-fat fryer, heat about 1¹/2–2 inches vegetable oil to sizzling. Cook the chicken wings, a few at a time, for 6–8 minutes or until golden brown and cooked through, no pink near bone. Drain on paper towels. Arrange on a serving platter and serve hot with chutney.

COOK'S FILE

Storage time: Chicken can be coated with spices several hours ahead. Store, covered, in the refrigerator.
Hint: Serve with a creamy dip such as ranch or blue cheese salad dressing along with crisp celery sticks.

CHICKEN BREASTS WITH CURRIED MANGO SAUCE

Preparation time: 10 minutes
Total cooking time: 15 minutes
Serves 4

4 boneless, skinned chicken
 breast halves (about 1 lb)
1 tablespoon vegetable oil
2 tablespoons butter
4 green onions, chopped

2 cloves garlic, crushed
1 tablespoon curry powder
1 teaspoon cornstarch
2/3 cup light chicken broth
1 large mango, peeled, seeded
 and puréed or half a 15 oz
 can mangoes, puréed
1/2 cup sour cream
2 teaspoons brown mustard
salt and pepper

TRIM CHICKEN of excess fat; rinse
and pat dry with paper towels.
1 In a large skillet heat oil and butter;
add chicken. Cook over medium heat
5–6 minutes on each side or until
lightly browned and cooked through.
Remove from pan; keep warm.
2 Add green onions, garlic and curry
powder to pan juices; stir over
medium heat for 1 minute.
3 Combine cornstarch and broth.
Add to skillet with puréed mango,
sour cream and mustard. Bring to a
boil, reduce heat; simmer 2 minutes
until slightly thickened; stir
occasionally. Season sauce, pour over
chicken and serve immediately.

1

2

3

SPAGHETTI WITH CHICKEN BOLOGNAISE

Preparation time: 10 minutes
Total cooking time: 15 minutes
Serves 4

2 leeks
1 sweet red pepper
1 tablespoon olive oil
1 lb ground raw
    chicken
2 cloves garlic, crushed
3 cups meatless spaghetti or
    marinara sauce
1 tablespoon chopped fresh
    thyme
1 tablespoon chopped fresh
    rosemary or 1–2 teaspoons
    dried rosemary
2 tablespoons seeded and
    chopped black olives
1 lb spaghetti
4 oz feta cheese, crumbled

salt and freshly ground black
    pepper

WASH LEEKS WELL. Cut into thin slices (white part only).

1 Finely chop the red pepper. In a large skillet, heat olive oil.

2 Add the ground chicken, sliced leeks, chopped red pepper and garlic. Sauté until the chicken is browned, stirring occasionally to break up chicken mixture.

3 Add the spaghetti sauce, thyme and rosemary. Bring to boil. Reduce the heat and simmer, uncovered, for 5 minutes or until sauce has reduced and thickened. Add the olives, stir to combine. Season to taste with salt and freshly ground black pepper.

4 Meanwhile, cook the spaghetti as directed on the package. Drain well. Place spaghetti on individual serving plates or pile into a large, deep serving dish and pour the Chicken Bolognaise sauce over. (Sauce can be mixed through the hot pasta.) Sprinkle with feta and serve immediately.

COOK'S FILE

Storage time: Chicken Bolognaise can be cooked up to 2 days in advance. Store, covered, in the refrigerator, or freeze for up to 4 weeks. Reheat the sauce and cook the spaghetti just before serving.

Variation: Any type of pasta, dried or fresh, is suitable to use. Freshly grated Parmesan or Pecorino can be used instead of feta cheese.

FETTUCCINE WITH CHICKEN AND MUSHROOM SAUCE

Preparation time: 10 minutes
Total cooking time: 25 minutes
Serves 4

2 large boneless, skinned
    chicken breast halves
    (about 8 oz)
1 tablespoon olive oil
2 tablespoons butter or
    margarine
2 slices bacon, cut into thin
    strips
2 cloves garlic, crushed
8 oz mushrooms, sliced
1/2 cup dry white wine
3/4 cup light cream
4 green onions, chopped
1 tablespoon unsifted
    all-purpose flour
1/4 cup water
salt and pepper
1 lb fettuccine
1/2 cup grated Parmesan cheese

TRIM CHICKEN of excess fat. Rinse
and pat dry with paper towels.

1 Cut chicken into thin strips. In
large skillet, heat oil and butter. Add
chicken and cook over medium-high
heat for 3 minutes or until browned.

2 Add the bacon, garlic and sliced
mushrooms; cook over medium heat
for 2 minutes more, stirring the
mixture occasionally.

3 Add the wine and cook until liquid
has reduced by half. Add cream and
green onions; bring to boil. Combine
flour and water until smooth. Add to
pan and stir over heat until the
mixture boils and thickens; reduce
heat and simmer for 1 minute. Season
to taste with salt and pepper.

4 In large saucepan, cook fettuccine
according to directions on package.
Drain. Add fettuccine to sauce and
toss to mix. Heat through. Sprinkle
with Parmesan. Serve immediately
with a green salad and hot herb bread,
if desired.

COOK'S FILE

Storage time: The sauce for this
dish can be made 1 day in advance.
Reheat sauce and cook pasta just
before serving.
Hint: Scrub cutting boards thoroughly
in hot soapy water to remove all
traces of chicken. Make sure wooden
boards have a smooth surface. Rough,
cracked surfaces can harbor bacteria.
Note: To make herb bread, combine
1/2 cup butter or margarine, softened,
with 1/2 cup chopped mixed fresh
herbs and a finely chopped garlic
clove. Slice a French or Italian loaf
diagonally; spread each piece with
herb butter. Reshape into a loaf, wrap
in foil and bake in a 350°F oven for
30 minutes or until loaf is hot.

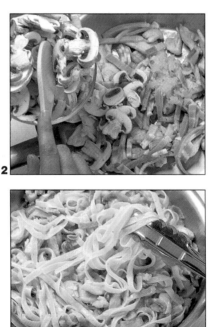

*Fettucine with Chicken and
Mushroom Sauce.*

CHICKEN DIANE

Preparation time: 10 minutes
Total cooking time: 18 minutes
Serves 4

8 boneless, skinned chicken
   thighs (about 1 1/2–2 lb)
2 tablespoons parsley
1/3 cup butter or margarine
2 cloves garlic, crushed

1 tablespoon Worcestershire
   sauce
3 tablespoons fresh parsley
1/2 cup sour cream
3 tablespoons light cream
salt and freshly ground black
   pepper, to taste

TRIM CHICKEN of excess fat and
sinew. Rinse chicken and pat dry with
paper towels.

1 Finely chop the parsley. In a large skillet, melt butter. Add the garlic and cook for 1 minute.

2 Add the chicken, cook on medium heat for 6–8 minutes on each side or until cooked through. Remove from pan and set aside. Keep warm.

3 Add the Worcestershire sauce, chopped parsley, sour cream and cream. Stir over medium heat for 1 minute. Season to taste with salt and pepper. Return chicken to pan, coat with sauce and serve.

1

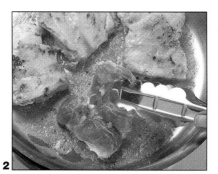

2

3

CHICKEN WITH GINGER PLUM SAUCE

Preparation time: 15 minutes
Total cooking time: 10 minutes
Serves 4

4 boneless, skinned chicken
   breast halves (about 1 lb)
2 tablespoons cornstarch
1/2 teaspoon Chinese five-spice
   powder
1 can (16 oz) purple plums,
   drained and pitted
1 cup water
1 tablespoon vegetable oil
2 medium onions, cut into thin
   wedges
2 stalks celery, sliced
   diagonally
1 tablespoon sesame oil
2 cloves garlic, crushed
2 teaspoons grated fresh ginger
1 small cucumber, halved
   lengthwise and sliced
1 tablespoon soy sauce
1 can (11 oz) lichees (litchis)
   drained

TRIM CHICKEN of excess fat and
sinew. Cut into 3/4-inch pieces.

1 In a medium bowl, combine
cornstarch and five-spice powder; add
chicken and toss until coated.

2 Place plums and water in blender
container or food processor bowl.
Blend or process for 10 seconds or
until smooth.

3 Heat vegetable oil in a wok or large
skillet. Add the chicken; stir-fry over
medium-high heat for 2 minutes until
brown. Remove and drain on paper
towels. Add onion, celery, sesame oil,
garlic and ginger; stir-fry for
2 minutes or until tender. Add
cucumber; stir-fry 1 minute.

4 Return chicken to pan with puréed
plums, soy sauce and lichees; stir
gently until sauce has boiled and
slightly thickened. Serve with steamed
rice, if desired.

COOK'S FILE

Storage time: Cook this dish just
before serving.

Note: Chinese five-spice powder is a
blend of Chinese brown peppercorns,
cinnamon bark, cloves, fennel and star
anise. Store all spices in an airtight
container in a cool dry place.

1

2

3

4

SESAME CHICKEN WITH TAHINI CREAM

Preparation time: 15 minutes
Total cooking time: 25 minutes
Serves 4

4 boneless, skinned chicken
    breast halves
    (about 1 lb)
1 tablespoon olive oil
2/3 cup fine bread crumbs
1/4 cup sesame seeds
1 tablespoon ground cumin
2 teaspoons chili powder
salt and freshly ground black
    pepper

Tahini Cream
1/2 cup Tahini
1/2 cup sour cream
1 tablespoon lemon juice
1 tablespoon finely chopped
    cilantro
2 green onions, finely chopped

PREHEAT OVEN to 400°F. Trim chicken of any excess fat and sinew. Brush fillets with oil.
1 Combine bread crumbs with sesame seeds, cumin, chili, salt and pepper. Coat chicken with mixture.
2 Place chicken on a lightly greased baking sheet. Bake for 20–25 minutes or until chicken is cooked through and lightly golden.

3 To make Tahini Cream: Combine Tahini, sour cream, lemon juice, cilantro and green onions; mix well. For a smoother sauce, place the mixture in a blender or food processor and process until smooth. Serve sauce with the hot Sesame Chicken.

COOK'S FILE

Storage time: Cook chicken just before serving. Tahini Cream can be made 1 day in advance. Store, covered, in the refrigerator. Bring to room temperature to serve.
Note: Tahini is a nutritious paste made from ground sesame seeds. It is available from most supermarkets, health food stores and delicatessens.

CHICKEN DRUMSTICKS WITH PESTO SAUCE

Preparation time: 10 minutes
Total cooking time: 25 minutes
Serves 4

1/2 cup pine nuts
1 cup firmly packed fresh basil
    leaves
1 cup firmly packed fresh parsley
2 cloves garlic, crushed
1/2 cup grated Parmesan cheese
3/4 cup sour cream or crème fraîche
2 tablespoons vegetable oil
8 chicken drumsticks
    (about 1 1/2–2 lb)

salt and pepper
1 cup water

PLACE PINE NUTS on a baking sheet. Broil 5 inches from heat for 2–3 minutes or until golden. Watch carefully; pine nuts color quickly so gently shake pan occasionally.
1 Place pine nuts, basil, parsley, garlic, Parmesan cheese and sour cream in food processor bowl or blender container. Process or blend until smooth. (Add some of the water if necessary). Pour into a bowl. Cover with plastic wrap and set aside.
2 In a large skillet, heat oil. Add chicken. Cook over medium-high heat for 15–20 minutes or until cooked

through, turning occasionally. Drain on paper towels; keep warm.
3 Wipe skillet with paper towels. Add pesto sauce to skillet; stir over medium heat until boiling. Season to taste. Pour over chicken to serve.

COOK'S FILE

Note: Crème fraîche is a matured, thickened, slightly fermented cream, available at most gourmet food stores. You can make it yourself by combining 1 cup whipping cream and 2 tablespoons buttermilk or sour cream in a glass container. Cover and stand at room temperature for 8–24 hours or until very thick. Store in the refrigerator for up to 10 days.

Sesame Chicken with Tahini Cream (top)
and Chicken Drumsticks with Pesto Sauce

SPECIAL OCCASIONS

CHICKEN TEMPURA WITH SEAFOOD

Preparation time: 25 minutes
  + 2 hours refrigeration & standing
Total cooking time: 20 minutes
Serves 4

3 large boneless chicken
    breast halves
    (about 12 oz)
1 tablespoon soy sauce
2 teaspoons sugar
1 tablespoon lemon juice
1¼ cups cornstarch
1 large egg, separated
⅓ cup water
6 oz scallops
8 oz medium shrimp
    in shells
¼ cup butter or margarine
¼ cup lemon juice,
    extra
2 teaspoons cornstarch
1 small red or green hot chili
    pepper, seeded and finely
    chopped
1 teaspoon instant chicken
    bouillon powder
¼ teaspoon dried oregano,
    crushed
1 tablespoon white wine
salt and freshly ground black
    pepper
⅓ cup vegetable oil

TRIM CHICKEN breasts of excess fat and sinew.

1 Cut each chicken breast into 4 long strips; place in a medium mixing bowl. Add combined soy, sugar and lemon juice; mix well. Cover with plastic wrap, refrigerate 2 hours. Combine cornstarch, egg yolk and water in a small mixing bowl; beat until smooth. Cover with plastic wrap and set aside for 1 hour.

2 Rinse and drain scallops. Peel shrimp, leaving tails intact; devein. In a large saucepan, melt butter; add seafood. Stir over high heat for 1–2 minutes or until cooked; remove seafood from pan and keep warm. Combine lemon juice, 2 teaspoons cornstarch, chili pepper, chicken bouillon, oregano and wine; add to pan. Stir over low heat 3 minutes or until mixture is smooth. Season to taste. Stir until mixture boils and thickens. Add cooked seafood to sauce; remove from heat. Keep warm.

3 Place the egg white in small, dry mixing bowl. Using a whisk, beat until soft peaks form. Fold egg white into cornstarch mixture. In a large skillet, heat oil. Dip chicken, a few pieces at a time, into batter; add to pan. Cook in batches over medium heat 2 minutes each side until just golden and tender. Drain on paper towels. Serve immediately with seafood and fresh vegetables.

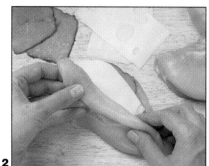

CHICKEN CORDON BLEU

Preparation time: 15 minutes
  + 30 minutes refrigeration
Total cooking time: 10 minutes
Serves 4

4 large boneless chicken breast
    halves (about 1 lb)
salt and pepper
4 slices Swiss cheese
4 thin slices smoked ham or
    pastrami

1/2 cup unsifted all-purpose flour
1 large egg, beaten
2/3 cup seasoned fine dry bread
    crumbs
2 tablespoons vegetable oil

TRIM CHICKEN of excess fat and sinew.

1 Using a sharp knife, cut a deep pocket in each breast half, cutting from thinnest into the thickest part without cutting through. Open out flat; season to taste.

2 Place a slice of cheese and ham on one side of each breast, cutting to fit as necessary. Fold remaining half of breast over to enclose filling, pressing to enclose ham and cheese.

3 Carefully coat each breast with flour; shake off excess. Dip into egg, then coat with bread crumbs. Place on a foil-lined baking sheet. Place, covered, in refrigerator for 30 minutes.

4 In large skillet, heat oil. Add chicken. Cook over medium heat 4–5 minutes each side or until chicken is golden and cooked through. (Add more oil if necessary.) Serve immediately.

SPICY STUFFED CHICKEN WINGS

Preparation time: 45 minutes
Total cooking time: 25 minutes
Serves 4

8 (1½ lb) large chicken wings
½ cup finely chopped water
   chestnuts
1 small onion, finely chopped
3 green onions, finely chopped
2 medium tomatoes, seeded
   and finely chopped
1 medium cucumber, finely
   chopped
½ cup chopped fresh cilantro
1 tablespoon chili sauce
salt, to taste
1½ cups soft whole wheat
   bread crumbs (2–3 slices)
2 tablespoons vegetable oil
2 red or green chili peppers,
   seeded and finely chopped
1 clove garlic, crushed

2 teaspoons curry powder
1 teaspoon ground cumin
1 teaspoon sugar
3 tablespoons lime juice
hot cooked noodles or rice

PREHEAT OVEN to 350°F. Wipe chicken and pat dry with paper towels.
1 Using a small sharp knife, start at cut end and slip knife down sides of bone towards joint, without piercing the skin.
2 Snap the bone free. Proceed with the next joint in the same way, taking care not to pierce the elbow. Remove the bones; reshape the wing.
3 Combine chestnuts, onion, green onions, tomatoes, cucumber, cilantro, chili sauce, salt and bread crumbs in a medium bowl; mix well. Divide into 8 portions. Using a spoon, stuff each wing with filling. Secure the ends with a toothpick.
4 In a large skillet, heat oil. Add chilies, garlic, curry powder and cumin. Stir over medium heat for 30 seconds. Add chicken; gently coat with spice mixture.

Cook over medium heat 2 minutes each side or until golden, but not cooked through. Transfer chicken to a shallow ovenproof dish. Add sugar and lime juice to pan juices. Stir over medium heat until well blended. Pour mixture over wings. Bake, uncovered, for 20 minutes or until tender. Serve hot, with pan juices as a sauce. Serve with noodles or rice.

COOK'S FILE

Storage time: This dish is best made just before serving.

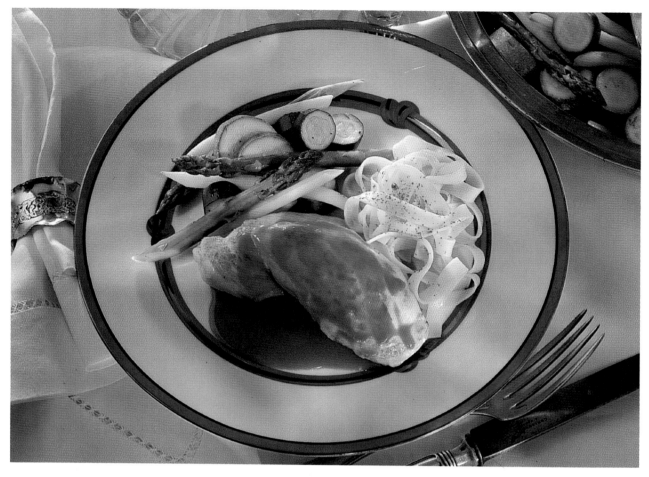

CHICKEN MARSALA

Preparation time: 5 minutes
Total cooking time: 25 minutes
Serves 4

4 boneless chicken breast
    halves (about 1 lb)
2 tablespoons vegetable oil
2 tablespoons butter or
    margarine
1 clove garlic, crushed
2¹/2 cups chicken broth or stock
¹/3 cup marsala wine
¹/3 cup light cream
2 tablespoons unsifted
    all-purpose flour

2 teaspoons Worcestershire
    sauce
salt and pepper

TRIM CHICKEN of excess fat and
sinew.
1 In a large skillet, heat oil. Add
chicken. Cook over medium heat for
5–6 minutes on each side or until
cooked through and lightly golden.
Remove chicken, cover with foil; keep
warm. Drain off any fat from pan.
2 Add the butter and garlic to the
pan; stir over medium heat for
1 minute. Add broth and marsala;
bring to a boil. Reduce heat and
simmer for 8–10 minutes or until the
liquid has reduced by half.

3 Combine cream, flour and
Worcestershire sauce; add to skillet.
Cook over medium heat, stirring, until
thickened, 2–3 minutes. Season to
taste. Pour over chicken. Serve hot,
with steamed vegetables and pasta.

COOK'S FILE

Storage time: Cook this dish just
before serving.
Hint: When cooking with wine, the
alcohol evaporates leaving just the
flavor of the wine in the food. Marsala
is a sweet wine and makes a sweet-
tasting sauce. Port or dry red wine
can be substituted, if desired. Another
option could be chicken thighs or
drumsticks for the chicken breasts.

1

2

3

BAKED CHICKEN ROLLS

Preparation time: 35 minutes
Total cooking time: 40 minutes
Serves 4

8 boneless, skinned chicken
    thighs (about 1 1/2 lb)
4 oz sun-dried tomatoes
3/4 cup shredded cheddar cheese
1/2 cup firmly packed fresh basil
    leaves
8 slices prosciutto or thinly
    sliced ham

Warm Mustard Dressing
1/3 cup olive oil
1 tablespoon balsamic vinegar
2 cloves garlic, crushed
2 teaspoons prepared mustard
Salt, to taste

PREHEAT OVEN to 400°F. Remove
excess fat and sinew from chicken.
1 Lay chicken thighs out, smooth-
side down, on work surface. Place a
sheet of plastic wrap over chicken and
pound with a meat mallet to 1/4–inch
thickness. Set aside.
2 In food processor bowl, combine
sun-dried tomatoes, cheese and basil.
Process just until finely chopped.
3 Spoon the tomato mixture onto the
end of each chicken thigh and roll to
enclose. Wrap each roll firmly in a
slice of prosciutto. Place rolls into a
shallow baking dish. Bake for
30–40 minutes or until cooked through.

Slice chicken and serve with Warm
Mustard Dressing.
**4 To make Warm Mustard
Dressing**: Combine olive oil, vinegar,
crushed garlic, mustard and salt in a
small pan. Stir over medium heat,
until hot.

COOK'S FILE

Storage time: Baked Chicken Rolls
can be assembled up to 2 hours ahead
and stored in the refrigerator. Cook
just before serving.

PESTO CHICKEN WITH FRESH TOMATO SAUCE

Preparation time: 30 minutes
Total cooking time: 25 minutes
Serves 4

4 boneless, skinned chicken
   breast halves (about 1 lb)
2/3 cup firmly packed fresh basil
   leaves
1/3 cup firmly packed fresh
   parsley
1 clove garlic, crushed
1 teaspoon finely grated lemon
   rind
2/3 cup slivered almonds, toasted
1/4 cup olive oil
2 tablespoons olive oil, extra

Fresh Tomato Sauce
1 tablespoon olive oil
1 medium onion, chopped
4 medium tomatoes, peeled,
   seeded and chopped

1 tablespoon tomato paste
1 teaspoon sugar
1/4 cup water
1 can (4 oz) pimiento, drained
   and chopped
salt and pepper

TRIM CHICKEN of excess fat and
sinew.
1 Lay chicken breasts smooth-side
down on work surface. Cover chicken
with plastic wrap and pound with
mallet to 1/4 inch thickness. Set aside.
2 In food processor bowl combine
basil, parsley, garlic, lemon rind and
almonds. Process until chopped. Add
1/4 cup oil slowly in a thin steady
stream, processing until all oil is
added and mixture is smooth.
3 Divide the pesto mixture between
the chicken breasts; spread mixture
evenly. Fold the fillets in half to
enclose the mixture. Secure with
toothpicks or skewers.
4 In a large skillet (or shallow baking
dish on stovetop) heat the

2 tablespoons oil. Add chicken. Cook,
over medium heat, for 4–5 minutes on
each side or until cooked through.
**5 To make Fresh Tomato
Sauce:** In large saucepan heat 1 tablespoon oil. Add onion; cook over medium
heat until just tender; do not brown.
Add tomatoes, tomato paste, sugar

and water; bring to a boil. Reduce heat; cook, covered, 3 minutes until tomato is soft but still holding its shape.

6 Add pimiento; cook until heated through, season to taste. Pour over chicken. Serve immediately with artichoke hearts or seasonal vegetables, salad and crispy bread.

COOK'S FILE

Storage time: Chicken can be prepared 2 hours in advance; cook just before serving. Sauce can be prepared 2 days in advance. Store, covered, in refrigerator; reheat gently just before serving.

Hint: To the toast almonds, spread on a baking sheet. Bake in 350°F oven for about 10 minutes or until they are lightly browned. To simplify, purchased pesto can be used in place of the fresh basil, parsley, garlic, lemon rind, toasted almonds, and 1/4 cup olive oil. Use 2–3 tablespoons pesto on each chicken breast and continue as above.

BLUE CHEESE CHICKEN WITH APPLE CHUTNEY SAUCE

Preparation time: 20 minutes
Total cooking time: 35 minutes
Serves 4

4 large boneless, skinned
    chicken breast halves
    (about 1 lb)
1/2 cup crumbled blue cheese
1/2 cup ricotta cheese
2 teaspoons Dijon mustard
1/3 cup chopped walnuts
1/4 cup butter or margarine,
    melted

Apple Chutney Sauce
1 tablespoon vegetable oil
1 leek, thinly sliced
2 cloves garlic, crushed
2 tart apples, peeled, quartered,
    cored and sliced
1/2 cup chutney
2 tablespoons finely chopped
    fresh chives
Salt and pepper

PREHEAT OVEN to 375°F. Trim chicken of excess fat and sinew.

1 Using a small, sharp knife, cut a deep pocket in each breast half, cutting from narrow edge into the thickest part of the chicken piece.

2 Combine blue and ricotta cheeses, mustard and walnuts in a medium bowl; mix well. Spoon into chicken pockets. Secure with toothpicks.

3 Place chicken in a shallow baking dish; brush with butter. Bake for 25–30 minutes or until cooked through and lightly brown. Remove toothpicks. Serve with Apple Chutney Sauce.

4 To make Apple Chutney Sauce: In a large saucepan, heat oil. Add leek and garlic; stir over medium heat 2 minutes or until leek is tender. Add apple; cook 4–5 minutes or until apple is tender. Stir in chutney and chives; season to taste. Stir until heated through.

COOKS FILE

Storage time: Chicken can be assembled up to 4 hours in advance, covered, and refrigerated. Cook just before serving. Apple Chutney Sauce can be made only one day ahead. Store, covered, in refrigerator.

ROAST CORNISH HENS WITH PEPPERCORN CHEESE SAUCE

Preparation time: 10 minutes
Total cooking time: 1 hour
Serves 4

2 Cornish hens
  (about 1¼ lb each)
2 large onions, cut into small
  wedges
2 tablespoons olive oil
freshly ground black pepper
⅓ cup brandy or cognac

1¼ cups chicken broth or stock
1 tablespoon chopped fresh sage
4 oz peppercorn cheese, cubed
salt, to taste

PREHEAT OVEN to 350°F. Remove giblets and any fat from the hens. Wipe and pat dry with paper towels.

1 Using poultry shears, halve hens lengthwise. Place onions into a shallow baking pan. Pour about half of the oil over; mix well. Sprinkle with pepper. Place hens, cut-side down, on onions. Brush with remaining oil.

2 Bake for 45 minutes or until the hens are golden and cooked through.

Remove the hens from the baking pan and keep warm.

3 Place the baking dish with onions on stovetop; add the brandy or cognac. Cook over medium heat until reduced by half. Add the broth and sage; bring to a boil. Add the cheese, reduce the heat and stir until cheese melts and the mixture is combined. Season sauce to taste. Place the hens on individual serving plates, pour over the Peppercorn Cheese Sauce and serve.

COOK'S FILE

Note: Peppercorn cheese is available at most specialty cheese stores.

1

2

3

MEDITERRANEAN CHICKEN

Preparation time: 20 minutes
Total cooking time: 45 minutes
Serves 4

4 boneless chicken thighs
    (about 14–16 oz)
2 tablespoons vegetable oil
1/4 cup black olives, pitted and
    chopped
2 cups cherry tomatoes, halved
2 cloves garlic, crushed
1 tablespoon chopped fresh
    thyme
salt and pepper
8 sheets phyllo, thawed
    according to package
    directions
1/3 cup butter or margarine,
    melted

Cream Sauce
2/3 cup heavy cream
1 teaspoon prepared mustard
1 tablespoon balsamic vinegar
3 tablespoons finely chopped
    fresh basil
4 oz feta cheese, crumbled

PREHEAT OVEN to 350°F. Trim chicken of any excess fat and sinew.

1 In large skillet, heat oil. Add chicken. Cook over medium heat 4 minutes on each side or until lightly browned and just cooked. Remove from pan; drain on paper towels.

2 Add the olives, tomatoes, garlic and thyme to the pan. Stir over medium heat for 1 minute or until tomatoes are tender but still holding their shape. Season. Remove from heat and cool.

3 Lay a sheet of pastry on a flat work surface. Brush chicken piece with melted butter and place on one corner of the pastry sheet; top with one-quarter of the tomato mixture. Roll up, tucking in the ends as you go. Place seam-side down in a lightly greased, shallow baking pan. Repeat with remaining pastry, chicken and tomato mixture to make four packets.

4 Bake, uncovered, 30 minutes or until golden. Meanwhile prepare Cream Sauce. Remove chicken from oven and place on a warmed serving platter or individual plates. Pour Sauce over and serve immediately.

To make Cream Sauce: In a small, heavy-based saucepan, mix together the cream, mustard and balsamic vinegar. Add the basil and feta cheese. Cook, stirring constantly, over medium heat until the sauce is heated through.

COOK'S FILE

Storage time: The chicken pieces and tomato mixture can be cooked 1 day in advance and stored, covered, in the refrigerator. Assemble Mediterranean Chicken and bake just before serving.

CHICKEN FLORENTINE WITH ROAST PEPPERS

Preparation time: 35 minutes
Total cooking time: 45 minutes
Serves 4

4 large chicken legs (drumstick and thigh, about 2½–3 lb)
½ package (10 oz) frozen chopped spinach, thawed
1 cup ricotta cheese
½ cup grated Parmesan cheese
3 cloves garlic, crushed
1 medium onion, thinly sliced
salt and pepper
¼ cup butter or margarine, melted
2 large sweet red peppers, halved, seeds removed

PREHEAT OVEN to 350°F. Trim chicken of excess fat and sinew.

1 Gently ease the skin away from the chicken meat, leaving skin attached on one side and forming a pocket.

2 Squeeze the excess liquid from the spinach. In a medium bowl, combine the spinach with ricotta, Parmesan cheese and garlic.

3 Spoon mixture carefully between skin and flesh of chicken. Use toothpicks to secure opening. Place chicken in shallow baking dish. Top with onion rings, salt and black pepper; drizzle with melted butter. Bake 45 minutes or until golden and cooked through.

4 Place peppers cut-side down on a baking sheet. Bake 30 minutes (in same oven with chicken) or until skin lifts away from flesh. Peel skin off peppers, slice and serve with chicken.

COOK'S FILE

Storage time: Chicken Florentine can be assembled a day ahead. Store, covered with plastic wrap, in the refrigerator. Bake just before serving. Roast peppers can be roasted a day ahead and refrigerated. Reheat the peppers in the oven while the chicken is cooking.

Variation: You can substitute whole Cornish Hens or chicken breasts with skin, for the chicken legs in this recipe. Make sure you adjust the baking time to suit.

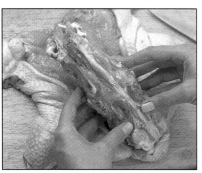

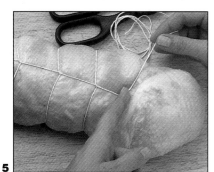

CHICKEN ROLL WITH ORANGE SAUCE

Preparation time: 1 hour +
  10 minutes standing
Total cooking time: 1 hour 45 minutes
Serves 4 to 6

1 broiler-fryer chicken
  (about 2¹/₂–3 lb)
3 oz dried apricots
6 oz ground or finely chopped
  fully cooked ham
1 cup fresh soft bread crumbs
1 cup cooked brown rice or
  brown and wild rice mix,
  cooked
¹/₂ cup shelled pistachio nuts
2 green onions,
  chopped
1 large egg, beaten
1 tablespoon canned green
  peppercorns, rinsed and
  drained (optional)
salt, to taste

Orange Sauce
1¹/₂ cups chicken broth or stock
2 tablespoons Grand Marnier (or
  other orange liqueur)
1 tablespoon finely shredded
  orange rind
4 teaspoons cornstarch
2 tablespoons orange juice

PREHEAT OVEN to 350°F.

1 To bone chicken: Cut through the skin along the center back. Using the tip of a small breast knife, separate flesh from bone down one side to the breast, without piercing the skin. Cut through the thigh and wing joint next to back.

2 Follow the bones closely with knife, gradually ease meat from the thigh, drumstick and wing. Scrape off the meat from bones and discard bones.

3 Repeat other side, then lift rib cage away, getting breast meat away from rib cage. Leave flesh and skin in one piece. Turn wing and drumstick inside chicken. Lay out flat, skin-side down.

4 To make Filling: Place the apricots in a small bowl; cover with boiling water. Stand for 10 minutes to soften; drain. Combine the remaining filling ingredients; press evenly over the chicken. Lay apricots in a line down the center, from one drumstick to the other.

5 Roll chicken, parallel to apricots, to enclose filling; tuck in ends as you go. Secure with toothpicks. Tie chicken at intervals with string to help retain its shape. Place on a rack in a baking dish. Bake 1¹/2 hours or until golden brown and cooked through. Remove from oven and keep warm, covered with foil.

6 To make Orange Sauce: Remove juices from baking dish; strain to remove solids. In small saucepan combine juices, broth, liqueur and orange peel. Bring to boil. Combine cornstarch and orange juice until smooth. Add to pan; cook and stir 2 minutes or until sauce boils and thickens. Remove from heat. Remove string from chicken, slice and serve chicken roll with Orange Sauce.

COOK'S FILE

Storage time: This dish can be assembled 1 day in advance.

Variation: Ground chicken or veal can be used instead of the leg ham in the filling.

CORNISH HENS IN RED WINE

Preparation time: 25 minutes
Total cooking time: 1 hour 10 minutes
Serves 4

2 Cornish hens (about 1¼ lb)
all-purpose flour
¼ cup olive oil
16 small boiling onions
4 slices thick-sliced bacon, cooked, drained and crumbled
2 cloves garlic, crushed
3½ cups red wine
⅔ cup brandy or cognac
4 bay leaves
1 tablespoon chopped fresh thyme
8 oz small fresh mushrooms
salt and pepper

REMOVE GIBLETS and any large deposits of fat from the Cornish hens. Rinse and pat dry with paper towels.

1 Using poultry shears cut hens into quarters. Toss lightly in flour; shake off excess.

2 In Dutch oven or heavy-based pan, heat oil. Add Cornish hen pieces. Cook for 2 minutes on each side or until lightly browned. Add onions, bacon, garlic, wine, brandy, bay leaves and thyme. Bring to boil, reduce heat. Cook, covered, 30 minutes. Stir occasionally.

3 Add mushrooms; continue cooking 30 minutes more or until hens are tender. Remove lid for last 15 minutes to reduce and thicken sauce. Remove hen pieces when done; keep warm. Boil mixture, uncovered, for about 5 minutes or to desired consistency. Season to taste. Serve red wine sauce with Cornish hens.

COOK'S FILE

Hint: Any robust red wine such as burgundy or claret would be ideal for use in this recipe.

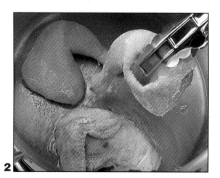

1

2

3

CHICKEN MOROCCO

Preparation time: 10 minutes
Total cooking time: 1 hour 5 minutes
Serves 4

4 large chicken legs (thigh and
    drumstick, about 2½–3 lb)
2 small onions
2 cloves garlic
1 tablespoon olive oil
2 teaspoons grated fresh ginger
1 teaspoon ground cinnamon
1 teaspoon ground cumin
1 teaspoon ground turmeric
2½ cups chicken broth or stock
1 tablespoon cornstarch
1 tablespoon water
¼ cup finely chopped fresh
    parsley
¼ cup finely chopped cilantro

½ cup lemon juice
12 green olives, pitted, chopped
2 teaspoons grated lemon rind
hot cooked couscous or rice

PREHEAT OVEN to 350°F. Trim
chicken of excess fat. Place chicken in
single layer in a shallow baking pan.
1 Chop onions finely. Crush garlic. In
a medium saucepan, heat oil. Add
onions, garlic and ginger. Cook over
medium heat 2 minutes or until onion
is tender.
2 Add cinnamon, cumin and
turmeric; cook 1 minute. Add broth;
stir until combined. Remove from heat.
3 Pour over chicken. Cover dish with
a lid or foil. Bake 1 hour or until the
legs are tender; turn occasionally.
Remove from oven; transfer to serving
plates or platter. Skim any fat from pan
juices; pour juices into small a pan.

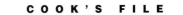

4

Combine the cornstarch and water;
add to mixture.
4 Stir in parsley, cilantro and lemon
juice. Cook, stirring constantly, until
mixture boils and thickens slightly.
Spoon sauce over chicken. Sprinkle
with olives and lemon rind. Serve
with couscous or rice.

COOK'S FILE

Storage time: This dish can be
cooked a day ahead. Store, covered, in
the refrigerator. Reheat for 30 minutes
in a moderate oven.

READY TO GO

recipes with take-out or pre-cooked chicken

CHICKEN SALAD WITH QUICK HERB DRESSING

Preparation time: 20 minutes
Total cooking time: none
Serves 4 to 6

1 whole cooked chicken
8 cups torn leaf lettuce
1 small cucumber, halved lengthwise and thinly sliced
1 sweet red pepper cut in thin strips
3 green onions
1/2 red onion

Quick Herb Dressing
1 cup sour cream
3/4 cup mayonnaise
1 tablespoon prepared mustard
1 tablespoon lemon juice
1 tablespoon chopped fresh chives
1 tablespoon chopped fresh thyme or lemon thyme
salt and freshly ground black pepper

REMOVE MEAT from the cooked chicken; discard the skin and bones.

1 Slice the green onions and cut the red onion into thin wedges.

2 Shred the chicken meat into bite-size pieces. Arrange lettuce on individual serving plates or in a large salad bowl. Place chicken, cucumber, red pepper, green onion and red onion on top of greens. Spoon Herb Dressing over salad. If desired, toss to mix. Serve salad immediately.

3 To make Quick Herb Dressing: In a bowl combine the sour cream, mayonnaise, prepared mustard and lemon juice; mix well. Stir in chives, thyme, salt and pepper to taste. Chill.

COOK'S FILE

Storage time: Chicken Salad can be assembled several hours ahead. Cover salad and store in the refrigerator. Add the Quick Herb Dressing just before serving.

Variation: You can substitute any of your favorite fresh herbs in the dressing for the chives and lemon thyme. Try using fresh cilantro, basil or tarragon. You could also try adding a clove of crushed garlic.

One-step Recipes

CHICKEN MELTS

Remove skin and shred meat from one-half of a cooked chicken (1½ cups meat). Using split English muffins or two slices Texas toast, spread with cream cheese. Top with chicken, sliced avocado and thinly sliced jarslberg cheese. Broil for about 3 minutes or until cheese is golden. Serve hot. Makes 2.

CHICKEN AND CORN SOUP

Remove skin and shred meat from one cooked chicken (3 cups meat). In a large saucepan, heat 3½ cups chicken broth. Add chicken, 8 oz can creamed corn, 8 oz can whole kernel corn, drained, 2 green onions, thinly sliced and ½ teaspoon soy sauce. Bring to boil; reduce heat and simmer 2 minutes. Season to taste. Serves 4.

CURRIED CHICKEN

Purchase one cooked chicken from your local deli or supermarket and cut into 8 or 10 pieces. In a bowl combine ¾ cup mayonnaise, 2 teaspoons curry powder, 1 teaspoon grated fresh ginger, 1 tablespoon lemon juice and 1 tablespoon chopped chives. Mix well. Arrange chicken pieces on lettuce; top with dressing. Sprinkle chopped walnuts on top. Serves 4.

ASIAN CHICKEN SALAD

Combine 3 tablespoons soy sauce, 3 tablespoons white wine vinegar, 1 clove garlic, crushed, 1 tablespoon fish sauce, 1 tablespoon lemon juice, 1 tablespoon chopped mint and 2 tablespoons chopped cilantro. Add 1 cucumber, sliced; 1 red pepper, cut in thin strips; 1 cup bean sprouts; and 1 small red onion, finely chopped. Add 3 cups shredded cooked chicken; toss to mix well. Serves 4.

CHICKEN NACHOS

Remove skin and shred meat from one-half of a cooked chicken (1½ cups meat). On a 12-inch pizza dish (microwave-safe) arrange a layer of tortilla chips. Spoon 1 can (15 oz) of refried beans over chips. Sprinkle chicken on top along with thin strips of green pepper. Pour over a jar (8 oz) of chunky taco sauce and top with 1½ cups shredded cheddar cheese. Heat in microwave on medium-high (70%) for about 5 minutes, turning occasionally, until cheese is melted. Serve hot, dolloped with sour cream or plain yogurt. Serves 4.

GRILLED CHICKEN SANDWICH

Remove skin and shred meat from one-half of a cooked chicken (1½ cups meat). Butter 4 slices of bread on one side, and spread the other side of two of the bread slices with Dijon-style mustard. On the mustard-topped bread slices, place chicken, thinly sliced tomato, thinly sliced ham or cooked bacon and the cheddar cheese. Sprinkle with pepper, if desired. Top with remaining slices of bread, buttered-side out. Grill on hot griddle 2–3 minutes on each side until golden. Serve hot. Makes 2.

CHICKEN SALAD

Remove skin and shred meat from one cooked chicken (3 cups meat). In a large salad bowl combine chicken, 1 cup halved cherry tomatoes, 1 stalk celery, thinly sliced, ½ cup small black olives, pitted and 1 small avocado, sliced (optional). For dressing, in a small jar combine ¼ cup olive oil, 2 tablespoons white wine vinegar, 2 teaspoons chopped fresh mint, salt and pepper. Cover; shake well. Pour over salad; toss to mix. Serve salad on lettuce leaves, if desired. Serves 4.

CLUB SANDWICH

Remove skin and shred meat from one-half of a cooked chicken. In medium bowl, mash ½ an avocado. Stir in ⅓ cup mayonnaise and 1 tablespoon brown or Dijon-style mustard. Toast four slices of rye bread. Spread mayonnaise mixture on one side of each slice of toast. Top two of the slices with chicken, sliced tomato, cooked bacon or thinly sliced ham or prosciutto and lettuce. Place remaining slices of toast on top, mayonnaise-side down. Cut diagonally. Makes 2.

CREAMY LEMON CHICKEN

Preparation time: 10 minutes
Total cooking time: 8 minutes
Serves 8

2 whole hot cooked chickens
1 lemon
¼ cup butter or margarine
⅓ cup unsifted all-purpose flour
2½ cups chicken broth or stock
¾ cup heavy cream

1 tablespoon chopped fresh chives
1 tablespoon chopped fresh basil
1 tablespoon chopped fresh parsley
salt and pepper

CUT EACH CHICKEN into quarters. Keep warm.

1 With a vegetable peeler, remove rind from the lemon. Slice rind into long, thin strips.

2 In a saucepan, melt the butter and stir in flour.

3 Combine the chicken broth, cream and lemon peel. Stir into pan. Cook and stir until smooth. Add the chives, basil and parsley. Stir mixture constantly over medium heat for about 4 minutes or until the mixture boils and thickens. Season to taste with salt and pepper. Pour sauce over chicken and serve immediately.

COOK'S FILE

Storage time: Lemon Sauce can be made 1 day in advance. Store, covered, in refrigerator. Reheat gently without boiling.

1

2

3

ORIENTAL CHICKEN AND NOODLE STIR-FRY

Preparation time: 15 minutes
Total cooking time: 10 minutes
Serves 4

5 oz dried flat Chinese noodles
   or egg noodles
1 cooked chicken
1 tablespoon vegetable oil
1 medium onion, cut in thin
   wedges
1 medium carrot, julienned
1 clove garlic, crushed
2 teaspoons curry powder
1/2 teaspoon crushed red pepper
1 large sweet red pepper, cut in
   thin strips
3 green onions, sliced
1/4 cup soy sauce
2 teaspoons sesame oil
1 package (6 oz) frozen pea
   pods, thawed

REMOVE MEAT from chicken and
discard the bones.
1 Slice the chicken into thin strips.
2 Cook the noodles in a large
saucepan of rapidly boiling water
until tender. Drain.
3 In large skillet, heat oil. Add onion,
carrot, garlic, curry powder and
crushed red pepper. Cook over
medium heat for 2 minutes. Add red
pepper strips and green onions. Cook
2 minutes more or until vegetables are
tender. Stir in soy sauce and sesame
oil. Add noodles, chicken and pea
pods. Stir-fry over medium heat for
4 minutes or until heated through.
Season to taste. Serve immediately.

COOK'S FILE

Storage time: Cook this dish just
before serving.
Variation: Any other vegetables can
be added to this dish.

1

2

3

CHICKEN PROVENCALE

Preparation time: 15 minutes
Total cooking time: 15 minutes
Serves 4

1 whole cooked chicken
1 tablespoon olive oil
1 medium onion, chopped
2 cloves garlic, crushed
1 large sweet red or green
 peppers, cut in thin strips
1 can (14½ oz) tomatoes,
 crushed
1 tablespoon tomato paste
⅓ cup dry sherry
½ teaspoon sugar

⅓ cup chopped fresh basil
 leaves
⅔ cup pitted black olives,
 halved
salt and pepper

REMOVE THE SKIN from the chicken if desired.

1 Cut the cooked chicken into 8 or 10 portions. Keep warm.

2 In a large skillet, heat the oil. Add the chopped onion, garlic and red pepper strips. Cook over medium heat until onion is tender. Add the undrained tomatoes, tomato paste, sherry and sugar. Bring mixture to a boil; reduce heat and simmer, uncovered for 10 minutes or until sauce thickens.

3 Add the chicken pieces, basil and olives to the sauce. Stir until heated through. Season to taste and serve immediately with a green salad and crusty bread.

COOK'S FILE

Storage time: Cook this dish just before serving.
Hint: Purchased, hot, cooked chickens should be eaten promptly. Whole chickens can be reheated in microwave. Remove from wrapping, place on a plate and cover with waxed paper. Microwave on Medium 5–6 minutes or until heated through. To reheat chicken pieces in conventional oven, preheat to moderately slow 315°F and cook for 25–30 minutes or until heated through.

ORANGE AND APRICOT CHICKEN

Preparation time: 10 minutes
Total cooking time: 10 minutes
Serves 4

1 medium orange
4 oz dried apricots
1 cup orange juice
2 teaspoons prepared
 mustard
⅔ cup chicken broth or stock
1 tablespoon cornstarch
¼ cup water
⅔ cup sour cream

1 tablespoon chopped fresh
 chives
1 whole cooked hot chicken
 (about 2–2½ lb)
salt and pepper

REMOVE THE RIND from the orange with a vegetable peeler and slice into thin strips. Cut the dried apricots into thin strips.

1 In a medium saucepan, combine dried apricot strips, orange juice and mustard. Stir over medium heat for 3 minutes or until the apricots are soft. Stir in the orange peel and the chicken broth or stock. Combine the cornstarch and water; add to the pan.

Cook and stir for 2 minutes or until the sauce boils and thickens.

2 Add the sour cream and chives and stir over low heat, without boiling, until the sauce is heated through. Season to taste.

3 Cut the hot cooked chicken into 8 or 10 portions. Place on a serving platter or individual serving plates. Pour the sauce over the chicken and serve immediately.

COOK'S FILE

Storage time: Cook this dish just before serving.
Variation: Add mango chutney or sweet chili sauce to the sauce.

Chicken Provençale (top)
and Orange and Apricot Chicken

CHICKEN AND PEPPERONI WITH PASTA

Preparation time: 20 minutes
Total cooking time: 15 minutes
Serves 4

1 whole cooked chicken
1 lb fusilli pasta
2 oz sliced pepperoni
1 medium green pepper
1 tablespoon vegetable oil
1 medium onion, cut in thin
   wedges
1/3 cup dry white wine
1/3 cup chicken broth
   or stock
2 teaspoons Dijon

1/4 cup heavy cream
salt and pepper

REMOVE MEAT from chicken. Cut chicken meat into strips and discard the bones.

1 Cook pasta in large pan of rapidly boiling water according to directions on package. Drain and keep warm.

2 Cut the pepperoni slices into thin strips. Cut the pepper into thin strips.

3 In a large , heavy-based saucepan, heat the oil. Cook onion, pepperoni and green pepper over medium heat for 2 minutes or until the vegetables are just tender.

4 Stir in the white wine, chicken broth or stock, Dijon mustard and cream; simmer gently for 2 minutes.

Do not boil. Add chicken; stir to heat through. Season to taste. Place the hot pasta in a large serving bowl. Pour chicken and sauce over; toss to combine. Season to taste with salt and pepper. Serve immediately with hot crusty bread.

COOK'S FILE

Storage time: Cook this dish just before serving.

Variation: Add sliced zucchini, mushrooms or pre-cooked green beans, if desired.

TOMATO CHICKEN CURRY

Preparation time: 15 minutes
Total cooking time: 15 minutes
Serves 4

1 whole cooked chicken
   (about 2–2¹/₂ lb)
1 tablespoon vegetable oil
1 onion, cut in wedges
2 cloves garlic, crushed
2 teaspoons grated fresh
   ginger
2 teaspoons curry powder

1 can (15 oz) crushed tomatoes
¹/₂ lb cauliflower, cut into small
   florets
2 stalks celery, sliced
2 tablespoons ground almonds,
   optional

CUT CHICKEN into 8 or 10 portions.
1 In large skillet heat oil; cook onion
and garlic over medium heat for
1 minute. Add ginger and curry
powder. Cook for 1 minute more.
2 Stir in the tomatoes, cauliflower and
celery. Bring to a boil. Reduce heat and
simmer, covered, for 5 minutes. Stir in
the ground almonds, if desired.

3 Add chicken to pan, stir to coat
with sauce. Simmer, covered, 5 minutes
or until heated through. Serve with
steamed rice, if desired.

COOK'S FILE

Storage time: Cook this dish just
before serving.
Variation: Fresh chicken pieces can
be used in this recipe. Trim off excess
fat, heat the oil and brown with the
onion, garlic, ginger and curry
powder. Add the tomatoes, cauliflower
and celery. Cover and cook over
medium heat for 30 minutes, until
tender. Continue as above.

1

2

3

CHICKEN AND ASPARAGUS GRATIN

Preparation time: 10 minutes
Total cooking time: 30 minutes
Serves 6

1 whole cooked chicken
1 can (15 oz) asparagus spears, drained
1 can (10¾ oz) condensed cream of chicken or mushroom soup
1 cup sour cream
2 green onions, sliced

1 medium sweet red pepper, cut in thin strips
salt and freshly ground black pepper
1¼ cups shredded cheddar cheese
⅔ cup grated Parmesan cheese
½ teaspoon paprika

PREHEAT OVEN to 350°F.

1 Remove chicken meat from carcass. Discard bones and slice chicken finely.

2 In a 10-inch quiche dish or large au gratin dish spread chicken in an even layer; top with half the asparagus. Combine the soup, sour cream, green onions and red pepper; season with salt and pepper. Pour over chicken.

3 Arrange remaining asparagus on top of the chicken mixture and cover with the cheeses. Sprinkle with paprika and bake for 30 minutes, until top is golden and mixture is bubbly. Serve immediately.

COOK'S FILE

Storage time: Cook this dish just before serving.

Variation: Use cream of corn soup or canned, creamed corn for a slightly different flavor instead of the chicken or mushroom soup.

1

2

3

INDEX

USEFUL INFORMATION

All the recipes in this book have been double-tested by our team of home economists to ensure high standards of accuracy. All the cup and spoon measurements used are level. We have used large (2 oz) eggs in all of the recipes. The sizes of cans available vary from manufacturer to manufacturer and between countries—use the can size closest to the one suggested in the recipe.

Glossary of Terms

Cook in batches: To cook in small, manageable amounts to ensure even cooking.

Cracked pepper: Small pieces of cracked peppercorns made in a coarse grinder. May be bought ready ground.

Devein shrimp: A process to remove the digestive tract using tweezers or by cutting a slight incision down the back after the shell is removed.

Dust: To lightly coat, usually just before serving and often with powdered sugar or cocoa powder.

Florets: The small heads of cauliflower or broccoli that are removed from the main stalk.

Garnish: An edible trimming on the dish to add color and enhance appearance.

Peeling tomatoes: To remove the skin from a tomato: mark a small cross on the bottom, then plunge the tomato into boiling water for 1–2 minutes. Then plunge into cold water. Peel skin down from the cross.

Process: To use either a food processor or a blender to finely chop or purée ingredients.

Simmer: To heat a liquid until small bubbles form and it is on the point of boiling.

Stir fry: To cook quickly in a little oil in a wok, stirring continuously.

Oven Temperatures

Cooking times may vary slightly depending on the type of oven you are using. Before you preheat the oven, we suggest that you refer to the manufacturer's instructions to ensure proper temperature control.

For convection ovens check your appliance manual, but as a general rule, you will need to set the oven temperature a little lower than the temperature indicated in the recipe.

	°F
Very slow	250
Slow	300
Warm	325
Moderate	350
Mod. hot	375
Mod. hot	400
Hot	425
Very hot	450

Cup Conversions

1 cup bread crumbs, dry	= $3^1/3$ oz
fresh	= $2^2/3$ oz
1 cup cheese, grated	
cheddar (firmly packed)	= 4 oz
mozzarella	= $4^3/4$ oz
Parmesan	= $3^1/3$ oz
1 cup all-purpose flour	= 4 oz
wholewheat	= $4^3/4$ oz
1 cup pasta, short (eg. macaroni)	= 5 oz
1 cup semolina	= 4 oz

Copyright© Text, design, photography and illustrations Murdoch Books® 1995.
All rights reserved under International and Pan-American Copyright Conventions.

No part of this book may be reproduced or transmitted in any form or by any means, electronic or mechanical including photocopying, recording, or by any information storage and retrieval system, without permission in writing from the publisher.

This 1997 Crescent edition is published by Random House Value Publishing, Inc.,
201 East 50th Street, New York, N.Y. 10022.

Random House
New York·Toronto·London·Sydney·Auckland
http://www.randomhouse.com/

Printed and bound in the United States of America

A CIP catalog record for this book is available from the Library of Congress
ISBN 0-517-18441-9

8 7 6 5 4 3 2 1